D0479710

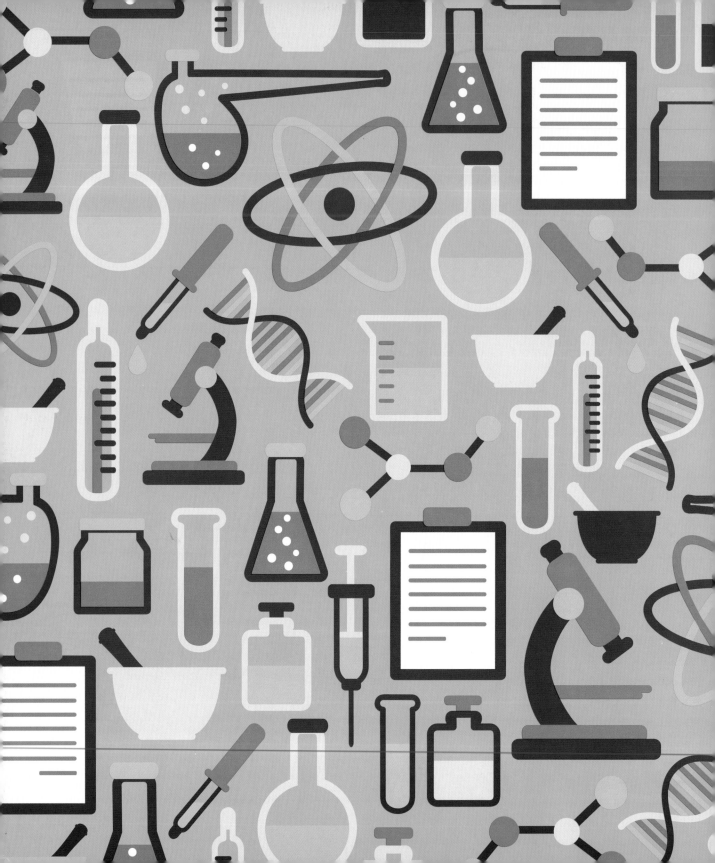

Smithsonian

10-MINUTE

SCIENCE EXPERIMENTS

Learn how to make your own Geyser Tube on page 48!

Science:
The Study of the Whole World

Have you ever wondered why certain things float, how explosions happen or what's going on when water freezes? It can all be explained through science! In each of these 50 experiments, you'll learn a little more about the world around you. And the best part is, most of these experiments will only take 10 minutes!

Table of Contents

Science Supplies
Most of these experiments call for common household objects, but two things you may need to stock up on are 1/4"-20 hex nuts (you can find these inexpensively at your local hardware store) and disposable pipettes (found online or at a local craft store).

Play With Food

Amaze Your Friends

Weekend Wonders

These experiments take more than 10 minutes, but they're worth the extra time.

The FUNdamentals

~~Don't~~ Do Try This at Home...

LET'S CUT TO THE CHASE AND BE HONEST—science experiments have changed over the years. OK, maybe the experiments haven't changed, but the way they're presented has. It seems all of today's science experiments come with a warning that reads, "Don't try this at home!" This is especially true when someone breaks out the vinegar and baking soda or anything else that might fizz, bubble, pop or get someone excited about learning.

What's the first thought that pops into your head when you hear, "Don't try this at home?" That's right... "I must do everything possible to try this at home!" The warning becomes a challenge for every young scientist who hears it.

Here's the good news: This book is filled with great science activities, demonstrations and science fair project ideas that are easy to do and guaranteed to get your creative juices flowing. And all of them can be done using materials you most likely have around the house! Don't be fooled by the list of simple materials required for many of the experiments—vinegar, eggs, plastic bags, salt, soap, etc.—even though they're basic ingredients, the "wow" factor of the activities is huge. At the end of each experiment, you'll learn the real science behind all of the "gee-whiz." You'll learn not only the "how" but the "why." And then something strange will happen—you'll start to ask your own questions and create your own experiments. Don't be surprised if a little voice in your head starts to ask things like, "What would happen if I changed this or tried that?" Curiosity will get the best of you and you'll find yourself doing the experiment again and again with your own changes and ideas.

And no matter what else you do, remember to make science fun!

-Steve Spangler

Science Safety

Science is a ton of fun, especially when you get to work with stuff like fire, knives, hammers and eruptions! But, of course, these are the same things that make an experiment a lot more dangerous. That's why it's so important to keep some safety steps in mind and carefully follow instructions whenever you're experimenting.

When experimenting, be sure to tie back long hair and wear closed-toe shoes.

Science Safety

1. ALWAYS ASK AN ADULT.

Before beginning any science experiment, ask your parent or guardian if it's **OK**. Even if the experiment doesn't involve anything unsafe, it's a good idea to get permission to use any supplies you need. Plus, you definitely should have an adult helping you if an experiment calls for lighting something on fire or using a sharp blade to cut things.

2. READ ALL INSTRUCTIONS.

Making sure you're ready and able to do everything an experiment calls for before you start helps ensure you stay safe and the experiment goes as planned.

3. WEAR PROTECTIVE CLOTHING, IF NECESSARY.

If you're working with anything that's bubbling, popping or about to explode, you should be wearing goggles! Heavy gloves are also necessary if you're working with hot objects.

4. WASH YOUR HANDS AFTER YOU'RE DONE EXPERIMENTING...

This is extra important if you're doing the Taco Sauce Penny Cleaner experiment on page 30!

5. ...AND DON'T TOUCH YOUR MOUTH OR EYES.

This is always good advice for keeping yourself from getting sick, but you definitely don't want to get any Crystal Tree solution (page 158) in your eyes.

6. NO EATING OR DRINKING IN THE LAB.

Or wherever you're doing your experiments. Again, you don't want to accidentally ingest anything unsafe!

If you want to conduct an experiment that you can eat, try out **Homemade Rock Candy (page 144)** or **Homemade Ice Cream (page 148)**.

The Scientific Method

Most of the experiments in this book are demonstrations of things scientists already know. But you can use the scientific method to turn any of these activities into an experiment that helps you understand even more about what's happening!

Science is the study of the world around us! In order to better understand how things work, we use the scientific method.

The Scientific Method

STEP 1 ASK A QUESTION

The first step is picking something you want to learn more about. For example, if you do the Floating Rice Bottle experiment on page 82, you might be wondering if the experiment would still work with other materials, like marbles, cotton balls or paper clips. You could even see if using different kinds of rice changes the outcome of the experiment.

STEP 2 GATHER INFORMATION AND OBSERVE

One of the best ways we can learn about something is to observe it. To continue the same example from before, you would spend a lot of time thinking about the other materials you want to try the Floating Rice experiment with. You might compare their weight, smoothness and size to grains of rice.

STEP 3 FORM A HYPOTHESIS

Once you've spent some time researching your other materials, you can make an educated guess about whether they will work as well as rice in that experiment. Scientists call this kind of "educated guess" a hypothesis.

STEP 4 LET'S EXPERIMENT!

Now there's nothing left to do but test your hypothesis! Recreate the experiment using the materials you've thought about, making sure you are changing only one thing at a time—this is called the variable.

STEP 5 ANALYZE YOUR RESULTS

Are the results what you expected they would be? (If they weren't, that's fine—you can use that information to come up with a new hypothesis.) Either way, make notes

A **constant** is a component of a scientific experiment that is always the same. A **variable** is a component of a scientific experiment that changes.

about how each material worked within the experiment.

STEP 6 DRAW YOUR CONCLUSION

Now that you have the results of your experiment, you can share them with the world! Write up what happened and why you think it did. If you're not sure why a different material did or didn't work, do some more research and keep experimenting!

DID YOU KNOW?

Scientists Francis Bacon (1561–1626), René Descartes (1596–1650) and Isaac Newton (1643–1727) all helped develop the scientific method.

Play With Food

GOBSTOPPER CANDY SCIENCE

FLOATING LETTERS

After these experiments you'll never look at food the same way again!

RED CABBAGE CHEMISTRY

WALKING ON EGGSHELLS

DISCOVER DNA!
Check out how to examine real DNA from a strawberry on page 38!

Gobstopper Candy Science

What happens when you dissolve these colorful candies in water?

MATERIALS

- White plate

- Room-temperature water

- Everlasting Gobstopper® candies

LET'S EXPERIMENT

Separate the Gobstoppers according to color and place three of each against the outside rim of a plate. They should be about equal distances from each other.

DID YOU KNOW?

This candy gets its name from British slang. In the U.K. and Ireland, "gob" means mouth.

2 Gently pour in enough room-temperature water to cover the bottom half of the candy.

3 Observe what happens over the next 5–10 minutes. What do you notice about the colors?

HOW DOES IT WORK?

Each Gobstopper is made up of four colors (and flavors), with a thin layer of wax between each color. Because of this, two important things happen in this experiment. First, thanks to the wax, the Gobstopper colors don't initially mix in the water. Instead, they run into each other and stop. Second, because of the multiple layers, the colors change during the dissolving process.

TAKE IT FURTHER

Repeat this experiment using hot water. Do you think the results will be the same?

Color-Changing Milk

Make your own mini, multi-colored Milky Way.

MATERIALS

- Milk
- Dinner plate
- Food coloring
- Dish soap
- Cotton swab

LET'S EXPERIMENT

Pour enough milk on the plate to completely cover the bottom to a depth of about 1/4 inch. Allow the milk to settle before moving on to the next step.

2 Add one drop of each of the four colors of food coloring—red, yellow, green and blue—to the milk. Keep the drops close together in the center of the plate of milk.

3 Use a clean cotton swab for the next part of the experiment. Predict what will happen when you touch the tip of the cotton swab to the center of the milk. It's important not to stir the mix—just touch it with the tip of the cotton swab. What happens?

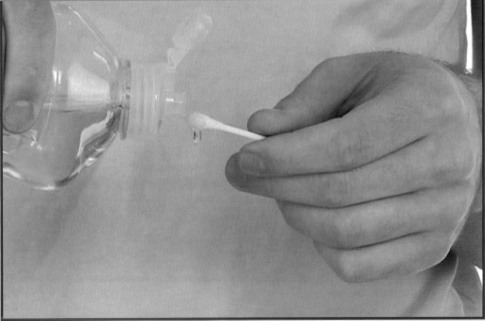

4 Now place a drop of liquid dish soap on the other end of the cotton swab. Place the soapy end of the cotton swab back in the middle of the milk and hold it there for 10–15 seconds. What happens?

Color-Changing Milk

5 Add another drop of soap to the tip of the cotton swab and try it again. Experiment with placing the cotton swab at different places in the milk. What do you observe?

HOW DOES IT WORK?

Milk is mostly water, but it also contains vitamins, minerals, proteins and tiny droplets of fat suspended in solution.

The secret of the bursting colors is in the chemistry of that tiny drop of soap. Like other oils, milk fat doesn't dissolve in water. When soap is mixed in, the HYDROPHOBIC portion of MICELLES break up and collect the fat molecules. Then the HYDROPHILIC surface of the micelle connects to a water molecule with the fat held inside the soap micelle. The molecules of fat move around in all directions as the soap molecules race around to join up with the fat molecules. During all of this fat molecule gymnastics, the food coloring molecules are bumped and shoved everywhere, providing an easy way to observe all the invisible activity. As the soap becomes evenly mixed with the milk, the action slows down and eventually stops.

A MICELLE is an electrically charged particle found in solutions like soaps and detergents.
HYDROPHOBIC means tending to repel water.
HYDROPHILIC means having a tendency to mix with or dissolve in water.

TAKE IT FURTHER

What do you think would happen if you tried this experiment using milk with a higher fat content?

DID YOU KNOW?

The average cow produces about 6-8 gallons of milk per day.

Candy Chromatography

MATERIALS

- Plate

- Coffee filter

- Black jelly bean

- Cup of water

Have you ever wondered how candies get their colors?

LET'S EXPERIMENT

1 Place a coffee filter on the plate, making sure it lays flat. Cut off the sides, if necessary.

2 Hold the black jelly bean in a cup of water for about 5 seconds.

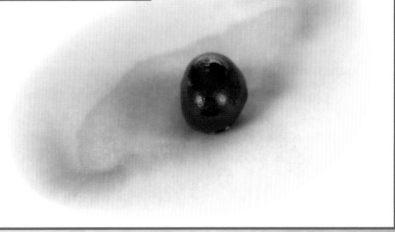

HOW DOES IT WORK?

Using a solid support (like paper) to separate different kinds of molecules is called chromatography. Scientists use this method all the time in different experiments.

Although the black jelly bean appears to be black, there are actually many different colored dyes that comprise the color. You can see the different dyes as they move up the filter paper. Some dyes are more attracted to the paper, while others are more soluble in water. Because of this, the dyes separate from each other and settle in varying distances from the jelly bean.

3 Place the black jelly bean in the center of the coffee filter and allow it to sit for about 10 minutes. What do you observe?

DID YOU KNOW?

President Ronald Reagan was a big fan of jelly beans and even sent them to astronauts on the space shuttle in 1983 as a special gift.

Floating Letters

They melt in your mouth but dissolve in water!

MATERIALS

- M&M's®

- Bowl

- Cup of water

LET'S EXPERIMENT

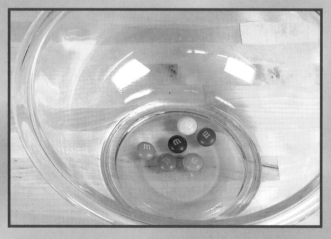

1 Place a few **M&M's®** in the bottom of your bowl. Keep each "M" facing up and spread them out as much as you can. They should be about equal distances from each other.

2 Slowly pour in room-temperature water in the bowl until the candies are completely covered.

3 Wait and observe the bowl over the next 10–20 minutes.

DID YOU KNOW?

M&M's® began being manufactured in 1941, but the candies didn't have "M" stamps until 1950. Even then, they were black-the company switched to white letters in 1954.

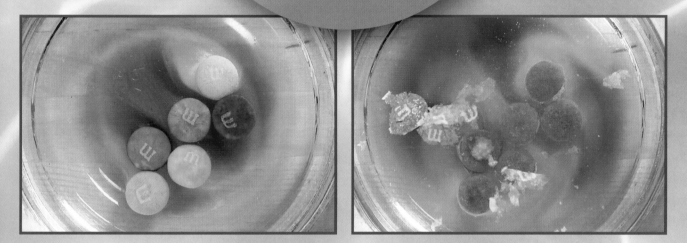

4 What do you observe?
Why do you think that happened?

HOW DOES IT WORK?

Some parts of **M&M's®** are water soluble, while other parts aren't. After a short time of soaking in the water, you begin to see the colored dyes from the **M&M's®** dissolve and mix together in the bowl. This lets you know the dyes are water soluble. However, the translucent shell and white "M" are not water soluble. That's why, after 10–20 minutes, you witness this hardshell and "M" float in the water without breaking apart.

Pop Rocks Expander

> Mix Pop Rocks® and soda to discover the secret behind the famous popping candy.

MATERIALS

- 16-oz bottle of soda
- Pop Rocks®
- Funnel
- Balloons

LET'S EXPERIMENT

1 The easiest way to get an entire package of Pop Rocks into a balloon is to use a small kitchen funnel. Place the narrow end of the funnel into the mouth of the balloon. Empty the Pop Rocks® packet into the funnel. Make sure the funnel is empty by giving it a few firm taps. You should be able to see into the balloon.

2 While keeping the balloon hanging down beside the bottle, stretch the opening of the balloon over the mouth of the bottle, making sure the valuable candy content doesn't get dumped into the soda. You don't want to drop the candy before you're ready!

3 Grab the balloon at its lowest point, lift it up and dump the Pop Rocks into the soda. Be sure to observe what's happening inside the bottle as the liquid reacts to the candies. What do you notice?

DID
YOU KNOW?

Before the invention of rubber balloons in 1824, people made balloons out of animal intestines.

HOW DOES IT WORK?

The secret behind Pop Rocks® candy is pressurized carbon dioxide gas (CO_2). When these tiny gas bubbles burst free from the candy, they make a popping sound. If Pop Rocks® are dropped into soda, which also contains lots of pressurized CO_2, some of the gas from the soda collects in gazillions of bubbles on imperfections, dents and bumps on the candy. The CO_2 escapes from the water and corn syrup that holds it and moves upward into the balloon.

29

Taco Sauce Penny Cleaner

MATERIALS

- Taco sauce

- Dirty pennies (at least 16)

- Small plate

- Vinegar

- Tomato paste

- Masking tape or sticky notes

- Water

- Salt

LET'S EXPERIMENT

Place several tarnished pennies on a plate and cover them with taco sauce. Use your fingers to smear the taco sauce all over the top sides of the pennies. Remember to wash your hands and not touch your eyes afterward. Allow the taco sauce to sit on the pennies for at least 2 minutes.

2 Rinse the pennies in the sink and look at the difference between the top sides of the pennies that touched the taco sauce and the bottom sides. Did taco sauce do the trick?

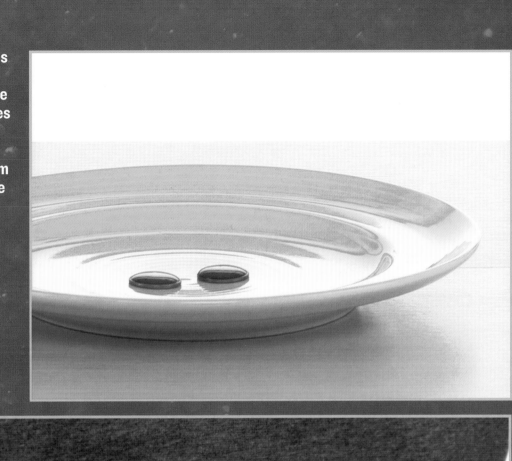

3 For an easy-to-see comparison, use another tarnished penny and carefully cover only half of the surface of the penny with taco sauce. Let the penny and sauce sit for a few minutes and rinse.

Taco Sauce Penny Cleaner

4 Take this experiment further by determining which of the ingredients in taco sauce is the cleaning culprit. The list of ingredients on a packet of taco sauce reveals four substances to test: vinegar, tomato paste, salt and water.

5 Place two equally tarnished pennies on each of four different plates. Use masking tape or a sticky note to mark each plate with the taco sauce ingredient you are testing (vinegar, tomato paste, salt or water). Cover the pennies with the various ingredients, smear them around with your fingers and allow the pennies to sit for at least 2 minutes. Be sure to wash your hands.

6 Rinse the pennies from each test plate with water. Did any of the pennies become clean?

7 Let's see if two or more of the ingredients work together to react against the copper oxide (the tarnish) on the penny. To test this, place two equally tarnished pennies on each of three different plates. Make three signs that say "Tomato Paste + Vinegar," "Salt + Vinegar" and "Tomato Paste + Salt." Cover the pennies with each of the respective mixtures, smear them around with your fingers and give the ingredients at least 2 minutes to react. Wash your hands.

8 Rinse the pennies under water. Which combination of ingredients results in the cleanest penny?

Test 1 — TOMATO PASTE + VINEGAR

Test 2 — SALT + VINEGAR

Test 3 — TOMATO PASTE + SALT

HOW DOES IT WORK?

The clear winner is the mixture of vinegar and salt. By themselves, the salt and vinegar do very little in the way of removing the coating of copper oxide on the penny, but together they make a great cleaning agent. When the salt and the vinegar are mixed together, the salt dissolves in the vinegar solution and breaks down into sodium and chloride ions. The chloride ions then combine with the copper in the penny to remove the tarnish, or copper oxide, from the surface of the penny.

So, the secret in taco sauce is the combination of the ingredients. Someone might argue that tomato paste is slightly acidic and may contribute in a small way to removing the copper oxide coating, but the real "power ingredients" are salt and vinegar.

TAKE IT FURTHER

How would you test the theory that tomato paste helps to remove the copper oxide?

DID YOU KNOW?

It's rumored Cleopatra won a bet to serve a wildly extravagant meal by dissolving pearls in a glass of vinegar and drinking it. It's hard to say if the story is true, but pearls do dissolve in vinegar.

Red Cabbage Chemistry

This activity is super smelly, but super cool.

MATERIALS

- Water

- Vinegar

- Blender

- Various containers

- Red cabbage
- Strainer
- Laundry detergent

LET'S EXPERIMENT

1 Peel off three or four big cabbage leaves and put them in a blender filled halfway with water. Blend the mixture on high until you have purple cabbage juice.

2 Strain the liquid into another container to separate out all the big chunks of cabbage.

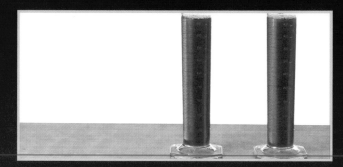

3 Set out two glasses side by side. Fill each glass 3/4 full with cabbage juice.

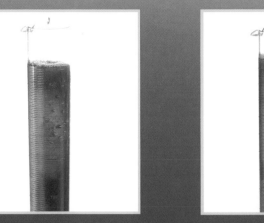

4 Add a little vinegar to the first glass of cabbage juice. After stirring, use the chart to determine if the liquid has an acidic, basic or neutral pH.

5 In the second glass, add 1 teaspoon of washing soda or laundry detergent. Again, use the chart to determine if the liquid has an acidic, basic or neutral pH.

DID YOU KNOW?

One of the earliest pH indicators invented was litmus paper. The paper is treated with 10-15 natural dyes that come from certain kinds of lichens. The earliest known use of litmus was by Spanish alchemist Arnaldus de Villa Nova around 1300 A.D.

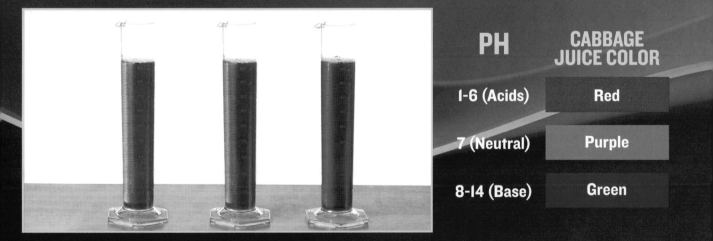

PH	CABBAGE JUICE COLOR
1-6 (Acids)	Red
7 (Neutral)	Purple
8-14 (Base)	Green

HOW DOES IT WORK?

Scientists measure acids and bases according to the pH scale. Acids have a low pH (0-6) and bases have a high pH (8-14). Neutral substances, like water, have a pH of 7. Scientists can tell if a substance is an acid or a base by using an indicator. An indicator is typically a chemical that changes color if it comes in contact with an acid or a base. Red cabbage contains a water-soluble pigment called anthocyanin that changes color when it is mixed with an acid or a base. See page 61 for more details on how acids and bases react when they're mixed together.

Walking on Eggshells

MATERIALS

Do you think you can walk across eggs without cracking them?

- 2–8 cartons of eggs
- Trash bags

DID YOU KNOW?

Joseph Coyle invented the egg carton in 1911 as a way to solve a dispute between a farmer and a hotel operator, who blamed the farmer for delivering broken eggs. Coyle designed a container made out of thick paper with individual divots that supported each egg from the bottom while keeping the eggs separated from one another.

THE COYLE EGG-SAFETY CARTON
IS THE CONTAINER THAT REALLY ELIMINATES YOUR
BREAKAGE PROBLEMS"

IT PAYS   EGG-SAFETY   IT PAYS

IT SAVES YOU MORE THAN ITS COST

Manufactured and Sold Only By
EGG-SAFETY CARTON CO.
S. HALSTED AT 49TH ST., CHICAGO

Egg-Safety CARTON

LET'S EXPERIMENT

Spread the plastic trash bag (or bags) out on the floor and arrange the egg cartons into two rows on top of them. Inspect all of the eggs to make sure there are no breaks or fractures in any of the eggshells. Make any replacements that might be necessary.

2 Make sure all the eggs are oriented the same way in the cartons. One end of the egg is more "pointy" while the other end is more round. Just make sure all of the eggs are oriented in the same direction. By doing this, your foot will have a more level surface on which to stand.

3 Remove your shoes and socks. Find a friend to assist you as you step up onto the first carton of eggs. Make your foot as flat as possible to distribute your weight evenly across the tops of the eggs. If the ball of your foot is large, try positioning it between two rows of eggs.

4 When your foot is properly positioned, slowly shift all your weight onto the "egg-leg" as you position your other foot on top of the second carton of eggs. There will be creaking sounds coming from the egg carton, but don't get nervous. Ask your friends to step away so that your full weight is on the eggs.

5 If you have more than two cartons of eggs, keep walking!

HOW DOES IT WORK?

The egg's unique shape gives it tremendous strength. The egg is the strongest at the top and the bottom (at the highest points of the arch). That's why the egg doesn't break when you apply pressure evenly to both ends. The curved form of the shell helps to distribute pressure evenly rather than concentrating it at any one point. However, eggs do not stand up well to uneven forces, which is why they crack easily on the side of a bowl—or when a chick needs to peck its way out!

Strawberry DNA

Learn how to extract and isolate real DNA.

MATERIALS

- Isopropyl alcohol

- Measuring spoons

- Water

- Dish soap

- Salt

- Strawberries

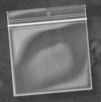
- Plastic bag

- Small beaker or clear cup

- Strainer

- Tweezers

- Medium bowl or beaker

- Measuring cups

- Dish

LET'S EXPERIMENT

1 Put a bottle of isopropyl alcohol in a freezer. We'll come back to it in Step 9. Measure 6 tablespoons (90 mL) of water into a small glass container.

2 Add 2 teaspoons (10 mL) dish soap to the water.

3 Stir in ¼ teaspoon salt and mix until the salt dissolves. This is the extraction mixture.

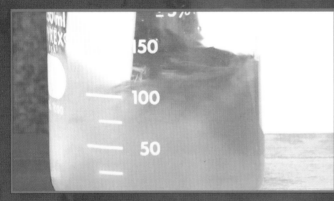

4 Place one strawberry into a plastic zipper-lock bag. Pour the extraction mixture into the bag with the strawberry.

DID YOU KNOW?

If you could unwind and straighten out the DNA molecules from just one of your cells, it would be 6 feet long. If you could do this with all of your DNA, it would stretch all the way to the sun and back multiple times!

5 Remove as much air from the bag as possible and seal it closed.

6 Use your hands and fingers to mash, smash and moosh the strawberry inside of the bag. You don't want any large pieces remaining.

7 Pour the resulting strawberry pulp and extraction mixture through a strainer and into a medium glass bowl or similar container.

8 Use a spoon to press the mashed bits of strawberry against the strainer, forcing even more of the mixture into the container. From the container it's in now, pour the extraction mixture into a smaller glass container that holds 1/4–1/2 cup (50–100 mL) of fluid. This will help to isolate the DNA on the surface of the mixture.

9 Add I teaspoon (5 mL) of the chilled isopropyl alcohol to the solution and hold the mixture at eye level. You're looking for a separation of material that shows up as a white layer on top. That's the **DNA** of the strawberry!

10 Use the tweezers to gently remove the **DNA** from the solution and lay it on a dish to examine.

HOW DOES IT WORK?

The long thick fibers you pull out of the extraction mixture are real strands of strawberry **DNA**. As you may know, **DNA** is present in every cell of all plants and animals and determines all genetic traits of the individual organism.

While other fruits are soft and just as easy to pulverize, strawberries are the perfect choice for a **DNA** extraction lab for two very good reasons: they yield much more **DNA** than other fruits and they are octoploid, meaning they have eight copies of each type of **DNA** chromosome.

(Human cells are generally diploid, meaning two sets of chromosomes.) These special circumstances make strawberry **DNA** both easy to extract and to see.

To extract the **DNA**, each component of the extraction mixture plays a part. Soap helps to dissolve cell membranes. Salt is added to release the **DNA** strands by breaking up protein chains that hold nucleic acids together. Finally, **DNA** is not soluble in isopropyl alcohol, especially when the alcohol is ice cold.

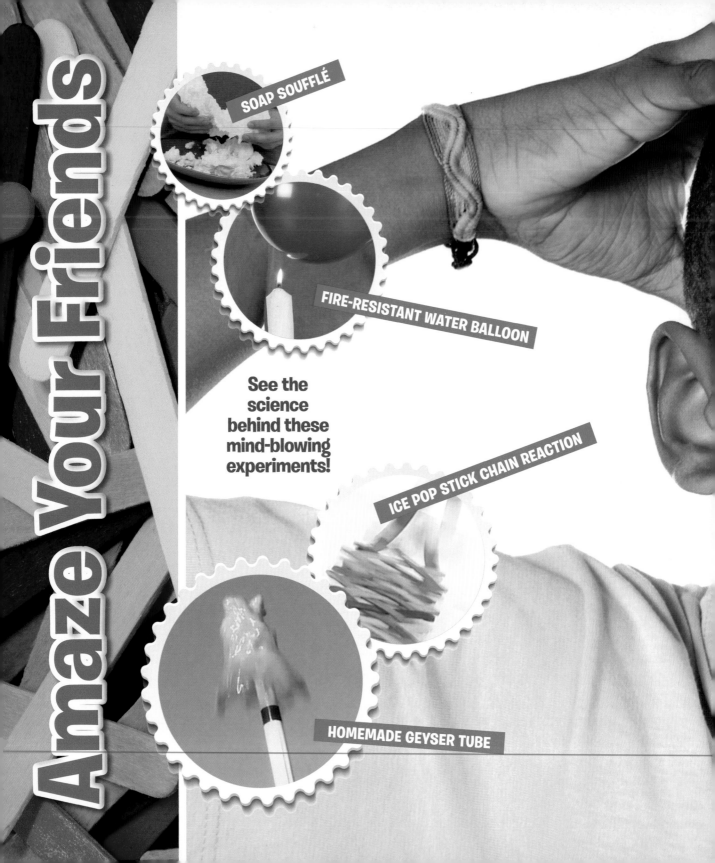

Amaze Your Friends

SOAP SOUFFLÉ

FIRE-RESISTANT WATER BALLOON

See the science behind these mind-blowing experiments!

ICE POP STICK CHAIN REACTION

HOMEMADE GEYSER TUBE

WOW!
Lots of these experiments can be done as "magic" tricks. Make sure to practice them before confounding your friends!

Ice Pop Stick Chain Reaction

MATERIALS

- Large ice pop sticks
- Clamp (or helper)
- Safety glasses

Get an up-close look at different kinds of energy.

LET'S EXPERIMENT

Start off with any two ice pop sticks. Lay them in an X-shape on a hard, flat surface that has a lot of room to work.

2 Place one end of a third ice pop stick under the end of the bottom stick and over the top stick of the "X." (See the yellow stick below.) Make sure to keep pressure on the center of the "X" as you work. That's why you need a helper or a strong clamp.

3 Repeat Step 2 with a fourth ice pop stick, but this time place it under the open end of the bottom stick and over the third stick. The second and the fourth ice pop sticks are now parallel to each other. Potential energy is building already and you can probably feel it. Keep that pressure on where the new "X" forms. The first "X" is now locked in place unless your helper (or clamp) lets go of the new "X".

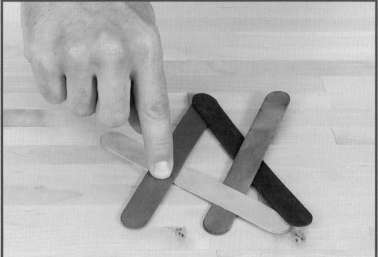

4 Continue adding ice pop sticks in this fashion until you have about 10–15 in a chain. Just remember it's a simple over-then-under that holds it all together and builds up energy.

Ice Pop Stick Chain Reaction

5 Once you've built the chain to your heart's content, release your clamp (or tell your helper to let go). The ice pop sticks explode down the line in a crazy chain reaction!

HOW DOES IT WORK?

The key to the ice pop stick chain reaction comes from POTENTIAL (or stored) ENERGY in the over/under weaving and KINETIC (or motion) ENERGY in the release.

As you weave the ice pop sticks together, you're gradually and continually building potential energy in the sticks. Each ice pop stick is slightly bent over a stick on one end and held under a stick on the other. This twisting and bending creates lots of potential energy in the wood fibers because it's not a normal position.

They want to return to a normal position and lose the added energy, but they can't. When you have the chain length you want, you let go. All of the potential energy is converted down the line in a chain reaction of kinetic energy!

POTENTIAL ENERGY is the stored energy an object has because of its position or state. **KINETIC ENERGY** is the energy of motion. Potential energy is converted into kinetic energy as it is used.

DID YOU KNOW?

Ice pop sticks were invented by accident–and by an 11-year-old! In 1905, Frank Epperson used a stick to stir soda mix into a cup of water, then accidentally left it outside overnight. When he found it the next morning, it had frozen into an icy treat with its own handle.

Homemade Geyser Tube

Build your own ignition device for this popular (and messy) experiment.

MATERIALS

- Safety glasses

- Roll of Mentos®

- 2-liter bottle of Diet Coke®

- Construction paper

- Toothpicks

- Electrical or duct tape

LET'S EXPERIMENT

Use the roll of Mentos® to roll the construction paper into a cylinder shape around the candy. You want the paper to be snug while still allowing room for the candy to be removed from it. Slide the candy out of the paper tube.

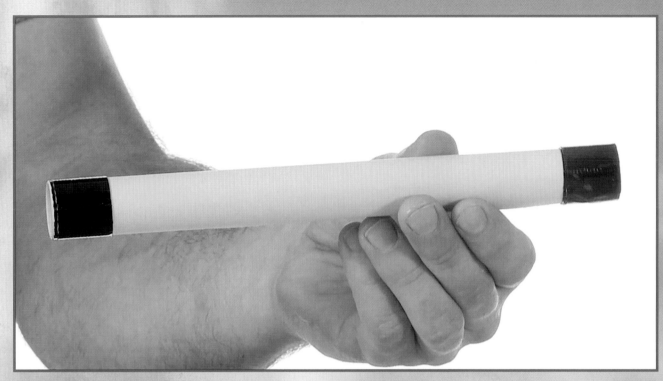

2 Tape both ends of the tube to securely hold the shape and size of the rolled paper. You may want to tape the edge of the paper too. (Leaving the Mentos® in the tube may make taping easier. Just remove the candy for the next step.)

3 Place one end of the paper tube into the mouth of the diet soda bottle. Make sure the bottom end of the tube is straight and smooth along its length. Also make sure the soda is still carbonated and hasn't gone flat.

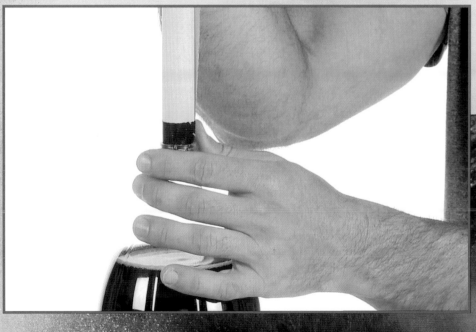

4 Hold the tube firmly in place with tape around the bottle opening.

5 Just above the tape by the opening, insert a toothpick straight through the paper. The toothpick needs to be centered in the tube and pierce both sides of the tube. Avoid making these two holes too large. The toothpick is the firing pin for the eruption.

6 GO OUTSIDE! Don't cause eruptions indoors. Drop 5–7 Mentos® into the top opening of the tube. When you're all set, slide out the toothpick and stand back! In a few seconds, the geyser will erupt.

DID YOU KNOW?
The proper word for an individual disc of the candy is dragee, pronounced "drah-jay." This comes from the French word dragée, meaning a sugar-coated pill.

HOW DOES IT WORK?

Water molecules are linked together around each bubble of CO_2 in the soda. To make the bubbles bigger, the water molecules must be forced away from one another. When you drop the Mentos® into the soda, the gelatin and gum arabic from the dissolving candy surface break the links of water molecules around the dissolved gas, so it takes less work for the gas to expand and form new bubbles. Each Mentos® candy has thousands of tiny micro-pits all over its surface too. These tiny pits are called nucleation sites and they're perfect places for CO_2 bubbles to form. As soon as the Mentos® hit the carbonated soda, bubbles form all over the surface of the candy. Plus, Mentos® candies are even more effective because they sink to the bottom of the bottle. That's a double whammy for making a geyser erupt. With the candy on the bottom of the bottle and the gas being released, it pushes all of the liquid up and out of the bottle in an incredible gas and liquid blast.

Five Divers

Bone up on buoyancy.

MATERIALS

- Scissors
- Glass of water
- 5 hex nuts

- 5 pipettes
- Empty plastic bottle with cap
- Permanent marker

LET'S EXPERIMENT

Using the permanent marker, number the pipettes I through 5.

2 Find a hex nut that fits snugly on a pipette and screw one onto each of the pipettes.

3 Cut each pipette just below the hex nut.

4 Squeeze the pipette to draw in or release water until the pipette barely floats in the drinking glass. Repeat with the remaining pipettes, trying to keep the amount of water in each pipette as equal as possible.

Five Divers

5 Fill the plastic bottle with water up to the rounded portion. Place pipette No. 1 in the bottle.

6 Squeeze three drops out of pipette No. 2 and place it in the bottle. Squeeze six drops out of pipette No. 3; nine drops out of No. 4; and 12 out of No. 5. Put each pipette into the bottle.

HOW DOES IT WORK?

When you have the water levels adjusted correctly in your pipettes, you should see the water in the pipette rise as you squeeze the bottle. The air trapped in the pipette compresses into a smaller space and the diver's weight increases. It becomes less buoyant and it sinks. When you release the squeeze, the compressed air expands and forces water out of the diver, allowing it to float to the top of the bottle.

So why do they sink one by one and float similarly?

It has to do with the drops of water you squeezed out before tossing your divers in the bottle. Keeping in mind how the divers work, each one reaches its buoyancy threshold with a different amount of pressure on the bottle.

7 Fill the remainder of the bottle with water and screw the cap on tight.

8 Squeeze the bottle and watch the pipette divers you've just made sink one at a time. Release your grip and you'll see the divers float right back to the top one at a time!

DID YOU KNOW?

The Cartesian Diver is a classic science experiment that's hundreds of years old. It's named for René Descartes (1596-1650), who made huge contributions in the fields of philosophy, math and science. The original Cartesian Divers were made out of glass medicine droppers or delicate glass ampules.

TAKE IT FURTHER

Do you think this experiment would be different in salt water? You could also do more tests with different amounts of air and hex nuts.

Soap Soufflé

Blow up a bar of Ivory® soap in the microwave.

MATERIALS

- Deep bowl (or plastic tub) of water

- Bar of Ivory® soap (must use Ivory® brand soap)
- Various bars of other soap brands

- Microwave

- Knife

LET'S EXPERIMENT

1 The first part of this experiment is designed to prove whether its claim to fame is true: Does Ivory® soap really float? Fill the bowl with water and drop in a brand-new bar of Ivory® to see for yourself.

2 Maybe all bars of soap float? If you have other brands of soap, try the float or sink test. You'll probably discover that all of the bars of soap sink except for the Ivory® brand soap. Why?

3 Remove the Ivory® from the water and break it in half. Make some observations about the shapes and textures inside the bar.

4 Use the knife to carefully cut the bar of Ivory® into four equal pieces. Place the pieces of soap on a dinner plate, then place the whole thing in the center of the microwave, after asking permission from an adult.

5 Cook the bar of soap on high for 1 minute. Don't take your eyes off the bar of soap— be sure to watch closely and make observations of what's happening. Be careful not to overcook your soap soufflé!

6 Allow the soap to cool for a minute or so before touching it. It's puffy but rigid! Don't waste the soap. It still works perfectly with a slightly different shape and size.

HOW DOES IT WORK?

Ivory® soap floats because air is whipped into the soap during the manufacturing process. If you break the bar of soap in half with your hands and look closely at the edge of the bar, you'll see tiny pockets of air. Those air bubbles in the soap contain water molecules. The expanding effect is caused when the water is heated by the microwave. The water vaporizes and the heat causes the trapped air to expand. Likewise, the heat causes the soap itself to soften and become pliable.

DID YOU KNOW?

The air-filled soap is believed to have been made by accident in the late 19th century by a Procter & Gamble employee who forgot to turn off the mixing machine. This caused so much air to be whipped into the soap that the batch nearly doubled in size. When the soap was formed into bars, they floated in water!

You need only one soap
IVORY SOAP

Pure...First quality.
Not expensive
Will wash anything
No chapping
IT FLOATS

57

Mysterious Water Suspension

MATERIALS

It's not magic–it's science!

- Empty clear soda bottle
- Plastic mesh screen
- Rubber band
- Toothpicks
- Pitcher of water

LET'S EXPERIMENT

Place the plastic screen mesh over the opening of the soda bottle. Secure it in place with a rubber band, then pour in water to fill the bottle.

2 Hold your hand over the mesh, then flip the whole bottle upside-down. Remove your hand. What happens? Is that what you expected?

3 Keeping the bottle vertical, push one toothpick through the mesh. What happens? Does any of the water run out?

4 Hold the bottle over the pitcher and tilt it until the water flows out. How do you think that happened?

HOW DOES IT WORK?

How does the water stay in the jar when your hand is removed? The answer is surface tension. The surface of a liquid behaves as if it has a thin membrane stretched over it. A force called cohesion, which is the attraction of similar molecules to each other, causes this effect. The water stays in the jar even though your hand is removed because the molecules of water are joined together (through cohesion) to form a thin membrane between each tiny opening in the screen. If you tip the jar at all, air will come into the jar and break the seal, causing the water to pour out.

You can even push a toothpick in without completely the surface tension, though you may have noticed a small drip of water coming out—it had to in order to make room for the toothpick.

TAKE IT FURTHER
Experiment with different screens. How does the size of the mesh affect the surface tension of the water?

DID YOU KNOW?
Surface tension is the reason why bugs such as water striders can walk on water.

CO$_2$ Extinguisher

You've probably never put out a candle like this before.

MATERIALS

- Safety glasses

- Vinegar

- Baking soda

- Clear container with a pour spout

- Lighter or matches

- Candle(s)

- Tray or cookie sheet

- Paper towels

LET'S EXPERIMENT

1 Place the clear container on the cookie sheet. Dump a couple of tablespoons of baking soda into the clear container.

2 Pour some vinegar in the container with the baking soda. It will foam a lot, but that's **OK**—you want it to overflow the container a little.

3 Let the reaction and the foaming calm down while you carefully light the candle(s). Hold the container next to and above the flame. Slowly tilt the container and "pour" just the gas from the container onto the flame. (Don't pour out the liquid.) The candle flame is no more!

HOW DOES IT WORK?

Fire requires oxygen (O_2), fuel and heat. Baking soda (sodium bicarbonate) is a base, and vinegar (acetic acid) is a weak acid. When they combine, the immediate reaction creates carbonic acid. But carbonic acid is very unstable and quickly decomposes into carbon dioxide (CO_2) and water (H_2O). The bubbles you saw in the container were full of CO_2. Because CO_2 is heavier than air, the container was filled with it and nothing else. As you tilt the container, you pour the CO_2 onto the fire. That means O_2 can't get to the fire and it goes out for lack of oxygen.

DID YOU KNOW?

Sodium bicarbonate is a super versatile salt used in medicine, food, cleaning, fireworks, fungicides, pesticides and fire extinguishers!

Twist in Time

Mix colors— and then separate them again.

MATERIALS

• Clear liquid dish soap

• 2 glasses (one must fit inside the other)

• 4 large or medium binder clips

• 3 small cups or bowls

• Food coloring

• 3 pipettes

• Water

LET'S EXPERIMENT

Add clear liquid soap to the larger of the two glasses until it is 1/3 full.

2 Place the smaller glass inside the large soap-filled glass.

3 Fill the smaller glass with water so the water is level with the top of the larger glass.

4 Clip three of the large binder clips around the rim of the larger glass. Make sure they are evenly spaced and leave a spot for the final clip to be added later.

5 Add a little soap to each of the three small cups and mix in two drops of food coloring. Each cup of soap needs to be a different color.

6 Use the three pipettes, one for each color, to add a small amount of colored soap to the clear soap inside the larger glass. Be sure to insert the colored soap below the surface of the clear soap.

7 Add the final binder clip to the empty spot of the larger glass.

8 Slowly rotate the smaller glass in one direction. You will see the colors begin to mix inside the soap.

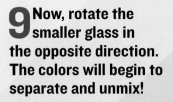

9 Now, rotate the smaller glass in the opposite direction. The colors will begin to separate and unmix!

HOW DOES IT WORK?

Believe it or not, scientists can't agree on why this happens! The most widely accepted explanation suggests that we are demonstrating something known as "laminar flow." Laminar flow occurs when a fluid flows in parallel layers. If the flow happens at a low velocity, or speed, the layers tend not to mix with one another. In this demonstration, the dyes remain within their original layers and do not mix with each other, even as they are spread out over their individual layers. Then as you turn the glass backward, the process is inverted almost perfectly.

DID YOU KNOW?

Two red food colorants, cochineal and carmine, are made from ground bugs.

Centripetal Force Penny

Put Newton's first law to good use.

MATERIALS

- Wire hanger

- Penny

LET'S EXPERIMENT

1 Bend the hook portion of the wire hanger to create a level surface for the penny.

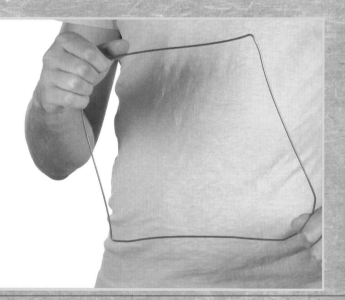

2 Stretch the hanger and open it up. The resulting shape should be very similar to a diamond.

3 Balance the penny on the hooked end of the hanger. (This might take a few attempts.)

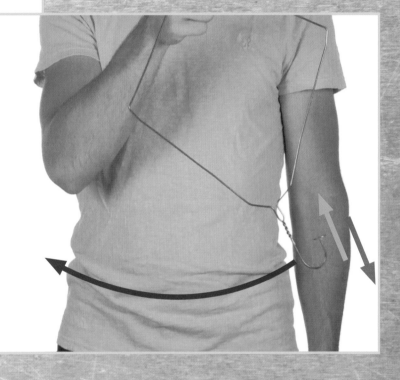

4 Begin to swing the hanger back and forth, starting with a very small amplitude (swing height) and gradually increasing the swing until you can spin it in a full circle. It might take a few times to get it right. But it is possible, and you can do it with practice!

HOW DOES IT WORK?

Any object moving in a circle is experiencing centripetal force. In this case, you are creating the force by swinging the hanger in a circle. According to Newton's first law of motion, objects in motion tend to remain in motion unless acted upon by an external force. Of course, gravity is acting on the penny and hanger too. But as you continue to swing the hanger, it "catches" the penny each time before it can fall—as long as you're swinging fast enough, that is!

DID YOU KNOW?

If you've ever ridden on a roller coaster that went upside down, you can thank centripetal force for keeping you in your seat!

67

Homemade Projector

With a cardboard box and a few simple steps, you can make a projector for your phone!

MATERIALS

- Smartphone with videos
- Utility knife
- Scissors
- Cardboard box (small, rectangular)
- Tape
- 2-inch (5-cm) magnifying glass
- Pen or marker

LET'S EXPERIMENT

Hold the magnifying glass against one of the "short" sides of the rectangular box. Position it in the center of the side but near the bottom edge. Trace around the lens of the magnifying glass with a pen or marker.

2 With the utility knife or sharp scissors, carefully cut out the circle you just drew. (Ask an adult for help!) Keep the edge of the cut as round and smooth as you can.

3 The phone needs something to lean against inside the box. Carefully cut off the short flap on the top of the box that's opposite the hole you just made.

4 Fold about a third of the flap downward so it looks like a ramp.

5 Slide the ramp portion under the short flap on the bottom of the box opposite the hole you cut. It should be a snug fit and the bottom flap should hold the ramp in place. The vertical piece of the ramp should be directly opposite the hole you cut in the middle of the box. It helps if it's as straight up and down as you can get. This is the location for the phone.

6 Securely tape the magnifying glass to the outside of the box over the hole you made. Don't tape over the lens!

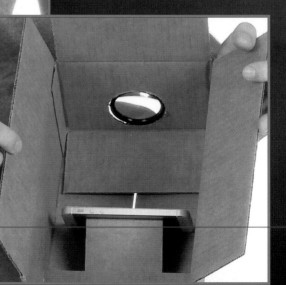

7 Lock the screen on your phone to a landscape orientation. Start playing a long video on the phone. Place it into the projector box so the images are upside down and lean it against the prop you installed. Close the box as tightly as you can with tape or lay a heavy book on top to make it as dark as possible inside the box.

8 Aim the box at your screen (a white wall), darken the room, grab a snack and enjoy the show!

HOW DOES IT WORK?

That image on the screen is much bigger than the lens in the magnifying glass! This works because of the shape of the lens and the fact that light travels in straight lines. A convex lens has a shape where the middle is thicker than the edges. The shape of a convex lens allows it to catch, bend and focus more light coming from the phone. The lens also flips the image as it passes through, which you've accounted for by turning your phone upside down.

DID YOU KNOW?

Historians believe the first magnifying glass was invented by philosopher Roger Bacon in 1250, though there is earlier evidence of crystal lenses being used for the same purpose.

Magic Spheres

MATERIALS

See if you can explain the science behind this "magic" trick!

- Clear container with lid
- Popcorn kernels
- Ping-pong ball

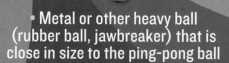

- Metal or other heavy ball (rubber ball, jawbreaker) that is close in size to the ping-pong ball

LET'S EXPERIMENT

Fill a tall, clear container ¾ with popcorn kernels. Push the ping-pong ball down into the kernels. Keep it in the center of the container, making sure no one can see the ball from any direction.

2 Set a metal or similarly heavy ball on top of the kernels and place the lid on the container.

3 Pick up the container and swirl and shake it gently. The metal ball will disappear and be replaced by the ping-pong ball!

HOW DOES IT WORK?

The two spheres share a comparable volume but differ greatly in mass. This means the balls have different densities. **DENSITY** is the measurement of how much "stuff" is packed into a measured space. Lower density always stacks on top of higher density. So what does density have to do with the metal ball sinking and the ping-pong ball rising? The swirling motion of the popcorn kernels (which have a density somewhere between the two spheres) allows the denser sphere to move downward and sink below the kernels. The same motion moves the plastic sphere upward. Individual kernels are sliding downward, below the ball, as it rises.

DID YOU KNOW?

When a popcorn kernel pops, its density changes! Popcorn kernels contain just a little bit of water, so when you heat them up, the water turns to steam and eventually "pops" the kernel as the pressure builds up. This increases the volume by a lot but only decreases the mass by a little, resulting in a lower density.

DENSITY
equals mass divided
by volume.

Static Flyer

MATERIALS

• Cotton towel

• Plastic produce bag

• Scissors

• Balloon

LET'S EXPERIMENT

1 Use a pair of scissors to cut a strip from the open end of the produce bag. Once the strip is cut, you should have a plastic band or ring.

2 Blow up a balloon to its full size and tie off the end.

3 Rub the cotton towel over the surface of the balloon for 30–45 seconds.

4 Flatten the plastic band on a hard surface and gently rub the towel on the band for 30–45 seconds.

TAKE IT FURTHER

Try using other objects to levitate the plastic band. Do some work better than others? What does this tell you about their charge?

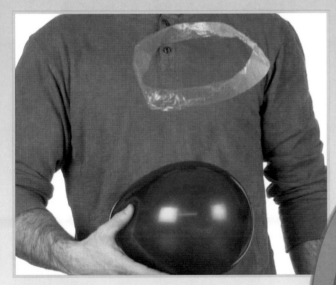

5 Hold the plastic band about 1 foot over the balloon and release it. The plastic band is levitating!

DID YOU KNOW?

"Static" means to stay in one place. That's why it's called static electricity–the charges are all staying in one area.

HOW DOES IT WORK?

Rubbing the towel against the balloon and the plastic band transfers a negative charge to both objects. The band floats above the balloon because the like charges repel one another. Similarly, when you rub a balloon on someone's hair, the balloon picks up electrons, leaving it negatively charged and the hair positively charged. Because opposite charges attract, bringing the balloon near the hair causes the hair to stand up.

Stuck Like Glue

Impress your friends with this science trick!

MATERIALS

Have an adult help you with this experiment!

• Plate

• Paper towel or napkin

• Bowl of water

• Wide-mouth jar

• Small piece of paper

• Lighter

LET'S EXPERIMENT

1 Trim or tear a paper towel (or napkin) into a shape that's bigger than the mouth of the jar or glass you're using. Dip the single layer of towel into the water to get it soaked. Shake off the excess water and smooth the wet towel onto the plate.

2 Tear off a piece of the paper roughly the size of a sticky note. Fold it, then (with an adult's permission) light it and drop it into the jar while it's burning.

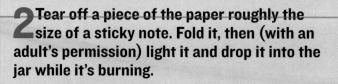

3 Make sure the paper is burning nicely in the jar. Then, carefully grab the jar, flip it over and place it upside down in the center of the soaked towel on the plate. Allow the paper to burn inside the jar until the flame goes out. Observe what happens where the rim touches the wet towel.

4 When the flame is gone, lift the jar— and see the plate be lifted up too!

TAKE IT FURTHER

Test what happens if you change the size of the burning piece of paper or the shape of the glass you use.

HOW DOES IT WORK?

The burning paper inside the jar is the cause of all this excitement. As it burns, it uses a little oxygen, but more importantly, the heat generated by the flame causes the air inside the jar to start moving very fast, to quickly expand and to leave the jar. With the jar upside down on the wet towel, you probably saw bubbles at places around the rim on the outside. That was expanding, heated air escaping the jar. With less air inside, the pressure in the jar drops.

When the burning paper goes out, the air inside the jar cools and contracts quickly. The wet towel blocks any returning outside air, keeping the lower-pressure air inside the jar and the higher-pressure air outside the jar. The difference between the two pressures is enough that the higher-pressure air outside pushes the plate against the lower-pressure air inside the jar.

DID YOU KNOW?

The amount of oxygen supply a fire has determines the color of its flame and how hot it is. Low-oxygen fires are relatively cooler and give off a yellow glow, while high-oxygen fires are hotter and burn blue.

Fire-Resistant Water Balloon

Balloons and flames don't mix... right?

MATERIALS

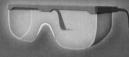

- Balloons
- Candles
- Lighter
- Safety glasses
- Water

LET'S EXPERIMENT   Have an adult help you with this experiment!

1 Blow up a balloon just as you normally would and tie it off.

2 Light a candle and place it in the middle of the table.

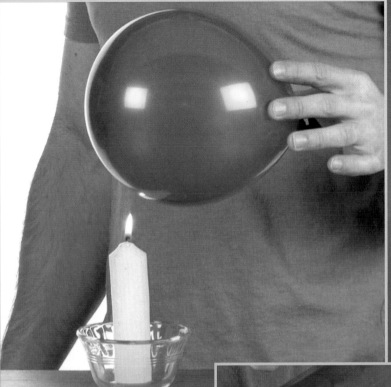

3 Put on your safety glasses because it's time to pop the balloon. With an adult's help, carefully hold the balloon a foot or two over the top of the flame and slowly move the balloon closer to the flame until it pops. You'll notice the flame doesn't even have to touch the balloon before the heat melts the latex and the balloon pops.

4 Fill another balloon with water, then blow it up with air and tie it off.

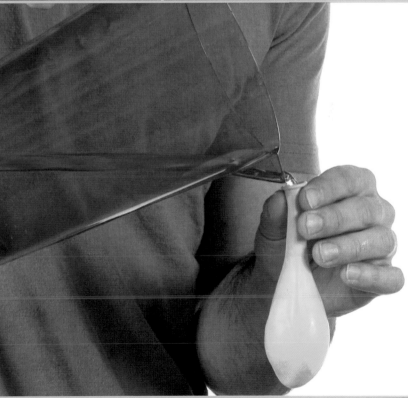

Fire-Resistant Water Balloon

5 Hold the water-filled balloon at the top while you slowly lower it over the candle—it won't pop. If you're very brave, you can actually allow the flame to touch the bottom of the balloon, but it still doesn't pop.

6 Remove the balloon from the heat and carefully examine the soot on the bottom. Why do you think the layer of water kept the balloon from popping?

HOW DOES IT WORK?

Water is a great substance for soaking up heat. The thin latex balloon allows the heat to pass through very quickly and warm the water. As the water closest to the flame heats up, it begins to rise and cooler water replaces it at the bottom of the balloon. This cooler water then soaks up more heat and the process repeats itself. In fact, the exchange of water happens so often that it keeps the balloon from popping until the heat of the flame is greater than the water's ability to conduct heat away from the thin latex.

The soot on the bottom of the balloon is actually carbon. The carbon was deposited on the balloon by the flame, and the balloon itself remains undamaged.

DID YOU KNOW?

Thanks to water's ability to soak up heat, people who live on the coast often live in more temperate conditions than those in land-locked areas! Water has a much higher heat capacity than soil or rock, so it takes longer to heat up and cool down than land does, helping regulate the area's temperature.

Floating Rice Bottle

This science trick is thousands of years old.

MATERIALS

- Long-grain rice

- 2 empty water bottles

- A friend

- Chopsticks

DID YOU KNOW?

In medieval China, sticky rice was added to lime mortar to increase its strength as a binding material for masonry.

LET'S EXPERIMENT

1 Fill two plastic bottles with rice. Stop when the rice is about an inch from the top.

2 Put the lid on one of the bottles and shake it. It should appear nearly full.

3 Tap the bottom of the second bottle on the table. As you tap, the rice will pack down in the bottle and make room for more. Add some more rice and continue to tap. You may even want to use one of the chopsticks to make a few jabs into the rice to pack it down even better. The important thing is to make both bottles look like they are full and have the same amount of rice in them.

4 Invite a friend to join you and give them the bottle with the fluffed up rice. Ask them to push the chopstick down to the bottom of the bottle. Do the same thing with your bottle of packed rice and the chopstick.

5 Have your friend gently lift their chopstick at the same time as you. Your bottle will be lifted up, but your friend's chopstick will slide right out.

6 Offer to exchange chopsticks and repeat the demonstration. Once again, it will work just fine with your bottle of packed rice, while your friend's bottle will remain on the table.

HOW DOES IT WORK?

When you insert the chopstick into the bottle of packed rice, it takes up additional space inside the bottle. Because rice is not fluid and has great difficulty moving up the neck of the bottle to compensate for the space the chopstick takes up, the packed rice tends to press against the sides of the bottle and the chopstick gets wedged in. Friction helps to hold the chopstick in the bottle as the bottle is lifted into the air.

Homemade Hand Boiler

Can you make water bubble with your own body heat?

MATERIALS

- Cup of water
- Handkerchief
- Rubber band
- Food coloring (optional)
- A friend

LET'S EXPERIMENT

1 Fill a small, clear drinking glass nearly full with water. Add a few drops of food coloring, if you'd like.

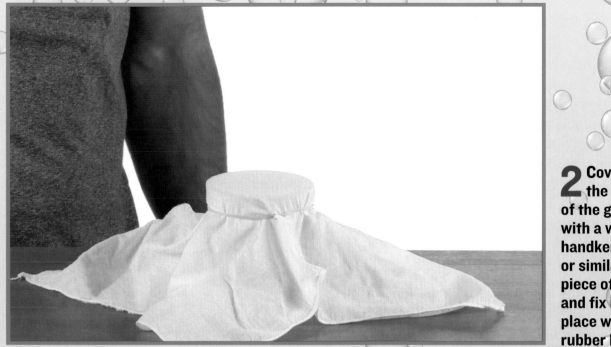

2 Cover the top of the glass with a white handkerchief or similar piece of cloth and fix it in place with a rubber band.

3 Place your hand over the cloth and quickly turn the glass over so the cloth is facing down and remove your hand. No water will come out.

Homemade Hand Boiler

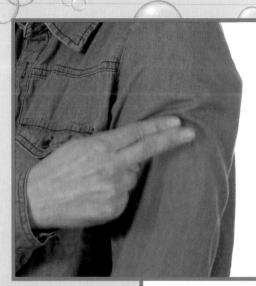

4 With the cloth still facing down, ask a friend to take two fingers and warm them up by rubbing them on their sleeve.

5 While your friend's fingers are below the cloth, push down on the glass with one hand while pulling up on the cloth with the other. (You might want to practice this a few times first.) The water inside the cup will begin to bubble!

HOW DOES IT WORK?

As you might realize, the water isn't boiling— it's bubbling. Bubbles are trapped air within a liquid, so that means there is air entering the cup and the water. Although the surface tension of the water and the cloth isn't letting any water out, air is getting in when you stretch the cloth. This is because molecules of air do not share the molecular bonds of water. Stretching the cloth pulls the holes in the cloth wider than normal and allows the air molecules to fill the little bit of space in the cup.

And if you're wondering why the water doesn't come out through the handkerchief, see Mysterious Water Suspension on page 58.

DID YOU KNOW?

Most handkerchiefs are square because of French King Louis XVI. It is said his wife, Marie Antoinette, disliked that there were handkerchiefs of varying shapes and sizes and had him decree their lengths and widths be equal.

Egg Drop

MATERIALS

Demonstrate the laws of motion for yourself.

- Water
- Metal pie pan
- Pint glass

- Raw eggs
- Empty toilet paper roll

LET'S EXPERIMENT

1 Pick a sturdy table or counter surface to perform the demonstration. Fill the drinking glass about ¾ with water and center the pie pan on top of the glass. Place the cardboard tube vertically on the pie pan, positioning it directly over the water. Carefully set the egg on top of the cardboard tube.

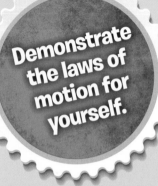

DID YOU KNOW?
The color of an egg's yolk depends on what plant pigments were in the hen's feed.

2 Stand directly behind the Egg Drop setup. Position your dominant hand about 6 inches away from the edge of the pan. The idea is to hit the edge of the pie pan with enough force to knock the cardboard tube out from under the egg. (It might take a few tries to get this right.) Gravity will do the rest as the egg falls directly into the glass of water.

TAKE IT FURTHER

Try testing longer cardboard tubes from a roll of paper towels, different size glasses or different size eggs. Do small eggs work as well as jumbo eggs?

HOW DOES IT WORK?

This can be explained by Newton's First Law of Motion. Newton said objects in motion want to keep moving and objects that are stationary want to stay still—unless an outside force acts on them. So since the egg is not moving while it sits on top of the tube, that's what it wants to do—not move. You applied enough force to the pie pan to cause it to zip out from under the cardboard tube (there's not much friction between the surface of the pan and the water container). The edge of the pie pan hit the bottom of the tube, which then sailed off with the pan. For a brief nanosecond or so, the egg didn't move because it was already stationary (not moving). But then, as usual, the force of gravity took over and pulled the egg straight down toward the center of the Earth.

Do Not Open Bottle

Create the ultimate prank with a 1-liter bottle and water.

MATERIALS

- Sharp pushpin
- Permanent marker, any color
- Water
- Clear plastic soda bottle (1 liter with cap)
- Towel to clean up your mess

LET'S EXPERIMENT

1 Clean and dry the 1-liter bottle and remove the label.

2 Fill the bottle to the very top with water and twist on the cap.

3 Use the permanent marker to write "**DO NOT OPEN!**" in large letters on the bottom half of the bottle.

DID YOU KNOW?

The word "plastic" comes from the Greek *plassein*, meaning "to mold or shape." Plastics are so moldable thanks to their molecular structure.

4 Carefully, use a sharp pushpin to poke a line of five or six holes about 1 inch (2.5 cm) from the bottom of the bottle. A small amount of water will squirt out as you poke holes in the bottle, but it's not a big deal. When you're finished, hold the bottle by the cap (don't squeeze the bottle or it will start leaking before you're ready) and give the bottle a gentle wipe down with the towel.

5 Carefully set the bottle on the kitchen counter (word-side out) where someone can see it as they pass by. Stay close enough to watch what happens. Let them unscrew the cap and you'll witness science in action. Water squirts everywhere!

6 As you test out your newly discovered water management skills, you'll quickly notice that it's funnier to watch people just pick up the bottle. Even the slightest squeeze on the sides as they lift the bottle results in water squirting from the holes.

HOW DOES IT WORK?

If the lid is on the soda bottle, air pressure can't get in to push on the surface of the water, and the tiny holes in the sides of the bottle are not big enough for the air to come in. In this case, the water molecules work together to form a kind of skin to seal the holes—it's called surface tension. If the lid is off, air enters through the top of the bottle and pushes down on the water (along with the force of gravity) and the water squirts out the holes.

Chemistry Rocket

Make your own tabletop rocket!

MATERIALS

- 3 pencils
- Scissors
- Strong tape
- 16-ounce bottle
- Safety glasses
- Rubber stopper
- Vinegar
- Paper towel
- Baking soda
- Tablespoon
- Funnel

LET'S EXPERIMENT

1 Use the scissors to cut about 12 inches (30 cm) of the strong tape from the roll. Duct tape is probably the best choice but you can use electrical or heavy masking tape as well.

2 Stick one end of the tape to the middle of the bottle, but don't wrap it around the whole bottle yet. Tape one pencil onto the bottle, letting about 2 inches (5 cm) of it extend beyond the opening of the bottle. Wrap the tape over the second pencil and then the third, making sure they're placed evenly around the bottle. Make sure the rocket is stable and points straight up on its three pencil legs.

3 Turn the bottle right side up and use the funnel to pour in some vinegar. You want the bottle to be about half full.

4 Grab a single paper towel from the roll. If there are multiple layers in the towel, separate them so you have just one thin layer. Keep the other layers for upcoming launches.

5 Tear the single layer into thirds or fourths and save the pieces for more tests.

6 Scoop a heaping tablespoon of baking soda and dump it into the center of the piece of towel you tore off.

7 Fold and wrap the towel around the baking soda to make a small cylindrical bundle. Don't tear the towel if you can help it. Grab the bottle, the bundle of baking soda and the stopper and take it all outside.

8 Outside, where you can make a mess safely and clean up with a hose, do the next five steps as quickly as possible to achieve a successful launch. (You might want to plan this out first.) You need to:
1. Push the paper towel–wrapped baking soda into the bottle.
2. Snugly twist the rubber stopper into place in the opening of the bottle.
3. Give the rocket a quick, hard shake.
4. Set the rocket upright on the pencils.
5. Stand back!

TAKE IT FURTHER
Test different quantities of baking soda and vinegar to lengthen the flight time and distance. You can test different sizes and shapes of bottles too.

HOW DOES IT WORK?

What happens when you mix vinegar with baking soda? There's a lot of bubbling and foaming! The bubbles and foam you see are filled with carbon dioxide gas (CO_2) that's being released by an acid/base reaction.

When you close the bottle with the rubber stopper, you prevent the CO_2 from immediately escaping the bottle. This causes a rapid increase of pressure inside the bottle. The pressure eventually gets to the point that the rubber stopper can no longer contain the gases and the stopper, and the contents of the bottle explode through the opening.

As the contents of the bottle shoot downward, the bottle itself shoots upward. This is a demonstration of Newton's Third Law of Motion: For every action, there is an equal and opposite reaction.

DID YOU KNOW?

The first rockets were actually fireworks! They were invented in China in 1232.

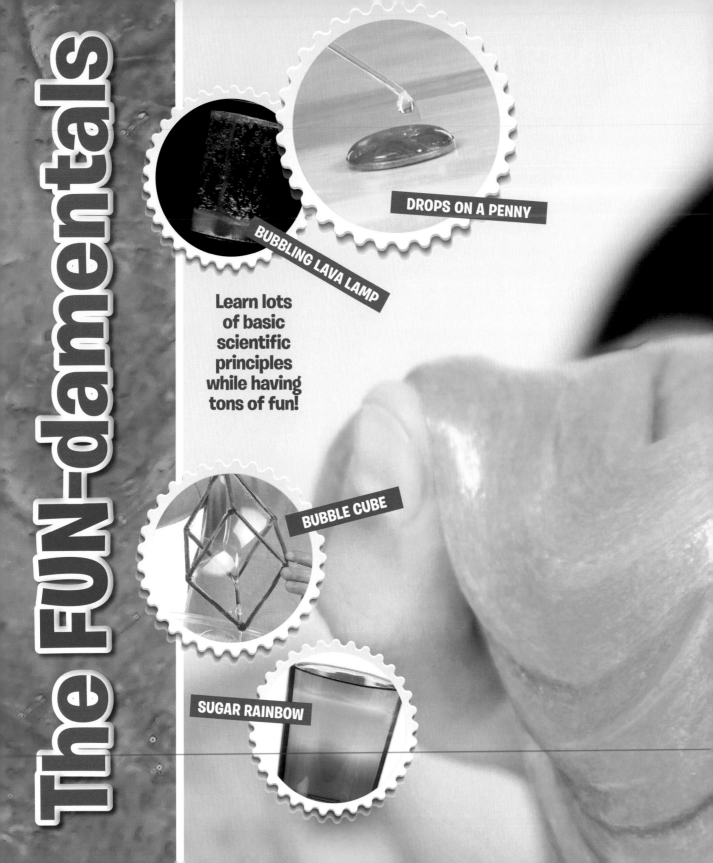

The FUN-damentals

DROPS ON A PENNY

BUBBLING LAVA LAMP

Learn lots of basic scientific principles while having tons of fun!

BUBBLE CUBE

SUGAR RAINBOW

SIMPLE SLIME!

Make your own ooey-gooey substance in just a few minutes! See page 102 to learn how.

Bubbling Lava Lamp

Make any room a little more groovy.

MATERIALS

- Food coloring

- Vegetable oil

- Flashlight (optional)

- Water

- Alka-Seltzer®

- Plastic bottle, vase or other container

LET'S EXPERIMENT

1 Fill the bottle or vase 1/8 full with water.

2 Add about 10 drops of food coloring. Make the water fairly dark in color.

3 Fill the rest of the container with vegetable oil.

4 To make a lava lamp, set the bottle directly on the lens of a large flashlight so the light shines up and through the liquid.

5 Divide the Alka-Seltzer® tablet into four pieces. Drop one of the tiny pieces into the oil-and-water mixture. (If using a flashlight, turn out the lights first!) Watch what happens. When the reaction slows, add another chunk of Alka-Seltzer®.

HOW DOES IT WORK?

There are two things going on in the experiment. One is the mixing of oil and water. The two do not fully incorporate into one another because they cannot form any chemical bonds with one another—oil molecules and water molecules are not attracted to one another.

The other important part is the adding of the effervescent tablet. The tablets contain sodium bicarbonate, which creates carbon dioxide when it meets water. This makes the bubbles you see within the bottle.

DID YOU KNOW?

The lava lamp was invented in 1963 by a British accountant named Edward Craven Walker. His original design used two different liquids which did not mix together: one water-based, the other wax-based.

Musical Straw

MATERIALS

Scissors   Straw

Feel how sounds are made!

LET'S EXPERIMENT

1 Flatten the top inch (25mm) or so of the straw with your teeth. Avoid curling the end of the straw up or down. Flatter is better, so bite down hard. You can also lay the straw on the table and press it down firmly with a spoon or knife along the two edges you created.

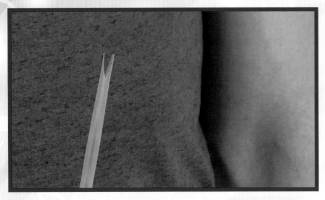

2 Cut off both corners of the flattened portion so it's narrower in the middle than the sides. These two flaps are where the vibrations that you hear as "music" will come from.

DID YOU KNOW?
Historians think the first rudimentary oboes were invented around 2800 B.C.

3 Place the cut end of the straw into your mouth, seal your lips around it and blow until a sound is produced. It's tough to do, so don't rush or blow too hard and long. The sound will be more of a squawk than music. You'll feel the entire straw vibrate as a sound is made too. Don't give up if you don't make a sound right away—you just need to reposition the straw and try again. There's a "sweet spot" where the sound occurs.

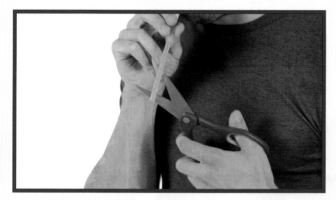

4 After you get the hang of making noise, carefully use scissors to cut short sections off the bottom of the straw while you're making the sound. Listen for rising changes in the pitch as you cut the straw shorter and shorter.

HOW DOES IT WORK?

When adjusted properly, the flattened end of the straw vibrates as the air you blow flows over it. These vibrations are passed onto the column of air inside the straw, which makes noise. This is similar to a double reed on some woodwind instruments. By cutting off pieces of the straw, you alter the length of the air column and change the pitch. An English horn, oboe and bassoon all use this same principle of double-reed vibration to make music. These instruments, however, change the length of the column of air with holes, stops and pads.

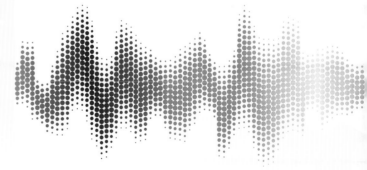

TAKE IT FURTHER
Use two different-sized straws, with one narrower than the other. The smaller straw should fit snugly inside the larger straw. On the smaller straw, repeat Step I. Slide the fatter straw over the thinner straw and start blowing. Move the larger straw back and forth to change the pitch of the sound by lengthening or shortening the column of air. It's a straw trombone!

Simple Slime

See the expanding power of fiber in action!

MATERIALS

- Food coloring
- Water
- Fiber powder (like Metamucil®)
- Oven mitts or gloves

- Microwave-safe bowl
- Measuring spoon
- Microwave
- Measuring cup

LET'S EXPERIMENT

1 Measure 2 cups (about 470 mL) of room-temperature water into a microwave-safe bowl. Add 2 teaspoons (1 mL) of fiber powder to the bowl of water. Add 2–4 drops of food coloring in the bowl. Stir it all together until the powder has completely dissolved.

2 Place the bowl of ingredients into a microwave. Cook on high for 2–4 minutes or until the mixture begins to boil.

3 Carefully remove the bowl using heavy gloves and stir the mixture before placing the bowl in the microwave again. Cook until it boils. Carefully remove the bowl from the microwave again and allow it to cool.

4 Once it has cooled, it's time for slime! Enjoy playing with your ooey-gooey, slimy snack.

HOW DOES IT WORK?

Fiber powder (like Metamucil®) contains an active ingredient called psyllium hydrophilic mucilloid. Psyllium is a soluble fiber, which becomes gel-like when it mixes with water.

DID YOU KNOW?

There are two kinds of fiber: soluble and insoluble. Soluble fiber dissolves in water, while insoluble fiber does not. Instead, insoluble fiber acts like a sponge, absorbing up to 15 times its own weight in water—this is why you feel full for longer when you eat foods with fiber!

Inseparable Books

MATERIALS • A friend • 2 notebooks

LET'S EXPERIMENT

1 Place the notebooks on a flat surface with the bindings facing inward.

DID YOU KNOW?
Paper is almost 2,000 years old! It was first invented in China in 105 A.D.

2 Open the covers, making sure they completely overlap with each other.

3 Alternate pages from each notebook placing one over the last, continuing until the notebooks are entirely intertwined.

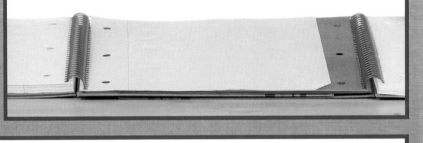

4 Holding the notebooks just inside the binding, have a friend pull on one of the notebooks while you pull the other. Pull as hard as you can. We bet you can't pull them apart!

HOW DOES IT WORK?

The reason you can't pull them apart is friction! You may think that the amount of friction between sheets of paper is pretty minimal, and when it's just a couple sheets, you'd be right. But when you multiply that friction by hundreds of surfaces—like each of the pages interwoven together—you wind up with an amount of friction that is insurmountable.

Sugar Rainbow

Understanding density has never been easier–or more colorful!

MATERIALS

- 6 tall, clear glasses (See NOTE in Step 1)
- Water (See NOTE in Step 3)
- Small dish or sink
- Turkey Baster
- Coloring tablets or food coloring
- Granulated sugar (You'll have great results with Imperial® Sugar or Dixie Crystals®.)
- Measuring spoons
- Clear drinking straw

LET'S EXPERIMENT

Fill each of the six glasses with water.
NOTE: The glasses need to be stable and about as deep as the straw is long. If you have shorter glasses, cut the straw to their length.

2 Use coloring tablets or food coloring to dye the water a different, bright color in each glass. You may need to mix the food coloring to make enough colors. Stir each glass completely.

3 The first of the six glasses will be just colored water with no sugar. The second color receives 1 rounded teaspoon of sugar. The third color receives 2 rounded teaspoons of sugar. The fourth gets 3 teaspoons and so on to 5 teaspoons of sugar in the last glass. Stir the solution in each glass until the sugar is completely dissolved.
NOTE: Using warm or room-temperature water will speed up this process.

Sugar Rainbow

4 Grab the straw and, if you haven't already, remove the wrapper. Hold the straw near one end, wrapping four fingers around the straw and placing your thumb over the straw's top opening.

5 To make your Sugar Rainbow, lift your thumb off the opening, dunk the lower end of the straw about I inch (3 cm) into the plain water. Cap the straw firmly with your thumb and lift it out of the water.

6 Dip the straw into the I teaspoon solution. This time, go twice as deep as you did into the first glass. With the straw in the liquid, lift your thumb but quickly replace it. Lift the straw and you'll have the first and second colored solutions in a stack inside the straw.

7 Continue the dipping process until you have all six colored solutions inside the straw. It's a density column of sugar water—a Sugar Rainbow!

8 To make an even bigger rainbow, use a turkey baster as a replacement for the straw to slowly layer the colored sugar solutions into a glass.

9 Draw in the liquid with the most sugar and add it to the glass.

10 Rinse the baster in fresh water. Draw in the liquid with the second-most amount of sugar. Hold the tip of the baster against the side of the container, close to the surface of the liquid already in the glass. Squeeze the baster gently so the water flows slowly down the side and then onto the previous layer.

11 Layer the rest of the sugar solutions in the same way. This can be hard to do but it's worth the effort when you finish. Make sure to take pictures!

DENSITY

is the measurement of how much "stuff" is packed into a measured space. Nearly every substance and material imaginable has a different density.

HOW DOES IT WORK?

By increasing the amount of sugar in the solution but keeping the amount of water constant, you create solutions that have increasing densities. The more sugar that's mixed into a measured amount of water, the higher the density of the mixture. As the Sugar Rainbow reveals, a solution with a low density stacks on top of a mixture with a high density.

DID YOU KNOW?

While humans will (sort of) float in an ocean, they float better in salty bodies of water like Utah's Great Salt Lake. It's so salty that it has a very high density, making it nearly impossible for humans to sink!

Electric Cornstarch

Find out how cornstarch goes with the flow.

MATERIALS

- ¼ cup cornstarch
- ¼ cup vegetable oil
- Balloon
- Spoon

LET'S EXPERIMENT

1 Pour 1/4 cup of cornstarch into a mixing bowl.

2 Add 1/4 cup of vegetable oil into the mixing bowl. Stir the mixture until it thickens.

3 Blow up a balloon and tie it off.

4 Statically charge the balloon using your hair, shirt or a rug.

5 Scoop up a spoonful of the cornstarch mixture and hold the charged balloon close to it. Once you witness the cornstarch jump toward the balloon, slowly move the balloon away. Repeat as many times as you want!

TAKE IT FURTHER

Try attracting the cornstarch to the balloon while it's in the bowl. What happens? How did the cornstarch act when you used the spoon as opposed to when you used the bowl?

HOW DOES IT WORK?

When you rub the balloon on a coarse surface like your hair, you give the balloon additional electrons. These new electrons generate a negative static charge. Meanwhile the cornstarch has a neutral charge. When an object has a negative charge, it will repel the electrons of other objects and attract that object's protons. When the neutrally charged object is light enough, like the dripping cornstarch in this case, the negatively charged object will attract the lightweight object.

DID YOU KNOW?

Combining 1.5-2 cups cornstarch with 1 cup water makes a substance called "oobleck," a non-Newtonian substance named after a Dr. Seuss story. Oobleck acts like a liquid if you pour it but behaves like a solid when a force is pressing on it.

Drops on a Penny

How many drops do you think you can fit?

MATERIALS

- Water
- Penny
- Pipette or eye dropper

LET'S EXPERIMENT

1 Wash and rinse a penny in tap water. Dry it completely with a paper towel. Place the penny on a flat surface.

2 Use an eye dropper or pipette to draw up water.

3 Carefully drop individual drops of water onto the flat surface of the penny.

4 Keep track of the water drops as you add them, one at a time, until water runs over the edge of the penny. You'll probably be surprised by the number of drops you get on there!

HOW DOES IT WORK?

Water's COHESION and SURFACE TENSION are special because of hydrogen bonds. Hydrogen bonds are formed by the hydrogen atoms of one molecule being attracted to the oxygen atoms of another molecule.

The cohesion and surface tension of water becomes apparent when the drops of water you add to the penny reach the penny's edge. Once the water has reached the edge, you begin to see a bubble or dome of water forming on top of the penny. The bubble shape is a result of the water molecules clinging to one another in an optimal shape (just like the bonds on the surface of a blown bubble).

IN GOD WE TRUST

DID YOU KNOW?
On average, 2009 pennies last 25 years.

COHESION
is the attraction of like molecules to one another.

SURFACE TENSION
describes the cohesion between water molecules.

Bubble Cube

Soap bubbles are always a perfect sphere—unless you help them take on a different shape.

MATERIALS

- 6 pipe cleaners
- Water, preferably distilled
- Glycerin (optional)
- 6 straws
- Scissors
- Large bucket or container (2-plus gallons, 7.5-plus liters)
- Dish soap
- Paper towels
- Pipette (or another straw)

LET'S EXPERIMENT

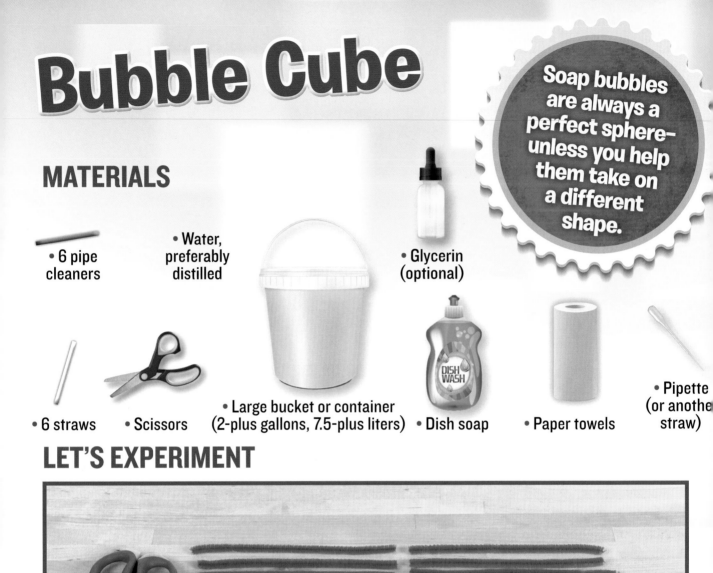

Use the scissors to cut each of the six pipe cleaners and straws in half. You'll have 12 pieces of each.

2 Twist three of the pipe cleaners together at an end to make a triangular, pyramid-shaped component. You'll end up with four, three-legged pieces.

3 Slide a piece of straw onto each pipe cleaner. Some of the pipe cleaner should stick out of the straw of each leg.

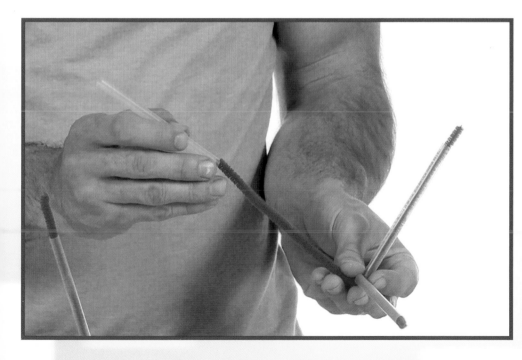

Bubble Cube

4 Build the cube by twisting the fuzzy wire ends on one component to the ends on another component. Connect the legs until the cube is complete. Make it as even a shape as you can.

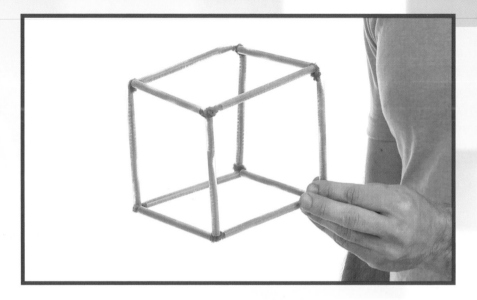

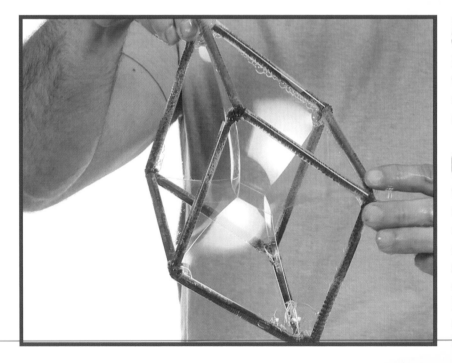

5 Mix the bubble solution. Check out the "Making Bubble Solution" directions on the next page. If using a pipette, cut off half the bulb end so you can use it to blow a bubble.

6 When the bubble solution is done, dip the cube into the solution. Let it sit for a few seconds and lift it out by holding on to two corners. Giving the cube a gentle shake helps the soap film even itself out and causes excess solution to drip back into the bucket. Set the cube on a flat surface to keep the bubble film stable.

7 Using your cut pipette or another straw, blow a bubble just above the center of the square. Voilà! When the bubble touches the center of the cube, it "magically" transforms from a sphere to a bulging cube.

MAKING BUBBLE SOLUTION

• Use a container that holds about 2 gallons (7.5 L) of water.

• Add approximately 1/4 cup (60 mL) of liquid dish soap. If you have hard water where you live, add extra. Real "bubble masters" prefer Dawn® dish soap, but other brands work too. Avoid dish soap that contains antibacterial products.

• If you have it, add a tablespoon of glycerin to your bubble mixture. Glycerin gives bubble film extra strength, but good quality glycerin can be pricey and perfectly good bubbles can be made without it. Some bubble recipes substitute clear Karo® syrup for glycerin due to the expense and scarcity of glycerin.

• Mix the bubble solution gently with your hand or a large spoon. For crystal-clear bubbles, be sure that you always keep the surface of the solution free of foam.

• Bubble solution improves with age. If you have the time, leave the mixture in an open container for at least 24 hours before using it.

HOW DOES IT WORK?

Bubbles use the smallest amount of surface area needed to enclose the air trapped inside. But as you dip the cube into the bubble solution, the solution stretches between the edges and the soap film clings to the sides of the cube (adhesion). This causes the bubbles to appear square or cubic. The soap film connects the shortest possible distance while still connecting all sides.

DID YOU KNOW?

Paintings of children playing with bubbles go back as far as the 17th century.

Balancing Hex Nuts

MATERIALS

- 4 soda cans
- 2 ceramic magnets
- Empty glass
- Ruler
- 5 hex nuts

A little magnetism can go a long way.

LET'S EXPERIMENT

1 Stack the soda cans two high at each end of the ruler. Set the ruler on top to bridge the towers.

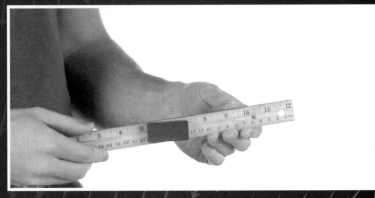

2 Place a magnet on either side of the ruler at its midpoint. The magnets need to attract and hold each other in place. The ruler should be sandwiched between them.

3 Set the ruler on top of the two towers so the magnets are centered. Place the drinking glass on the table between the towers so a point on the rim of the glass is centered below the magnets.

4 Attach the hex nuts to the magnet underneath the ruler so one hex nut is connected to another in a hanging column. Build it as straight as you can.

5 Slowly detach the column of hex nuts from the magnet and lower it to the rim of the glass directly under the magnet. Balance the stack on the rim of the glass very carefully. Make sure the hex nuts are directly below the magnet on the rim of the glass. This may take a few attempts, but you'll get it.

HOW DOES IT WORK?

As you attach each hex nut to the magnet, it's easy to see that the magnets are causing them to attract and hold on to each other. While the hex nuts are in contact with the magnet, they develop their own internal magnetic field. These weak magnetic fields will remain after you detach the hex nuts from the magnets.

When you balance the hex nuts on the edge of the drinking glass below the magnets, they still have a little bit of that magnetism left. This weak field is just enough to attract the hex nuts to the overhead magnets' much stronger field. As you'd expect, they remain as a wobbly stack until the magnets are removed. After that, gravity takes over!

DID YOU KNOW?

The Earth is a giant magnet! Its solid-iron core is surrounded by molten iron, which creates a magnetic field around the planet.

TAKE IT FURTHER
How many hex nuts can you stack?

Floating Ping-Pong Ball

Find out what's "up" with Bernoulli's Principle.

MATERIALS

- Adult supervision
- Tape
- Large nail

- Utility blade
- Bendy straw
- Ping-pong ball
- Hammer
- 1-liter bottle with cap

LET'S EXPERIMENT

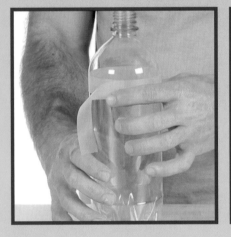

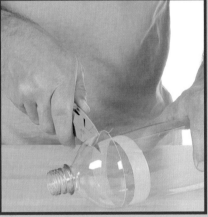

1 Near the top of a 1-liter bottle, just before the sides start to curve inward, wrap a piece of tape. Try to wrap the tape as straight as possible around the entire circumference of the bottle.

2 With adult help, use the tape as a guide to cut the top of the bottle off with the box cutter. Again, try to make your cut as straight as possible.

3 Find a work bench or similar surface and ask an adult for help. Place the bottle cap, open side down, onto the work bench. Center a large nail on the top of the bottle cap and use a hammer to punch a hole in the cap. Pull the nail out of the bottle cap and you should have a nice, round hole.

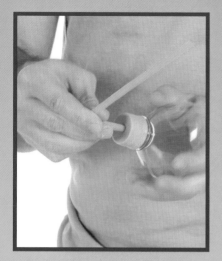  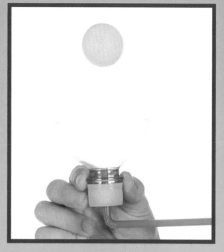

4 Test the bottle cap to see if a bendy straw will fit snugly in the hole you've created.

If the hole is too small, find a larger nail and widen the hole. If the hole is too large, wrap tape around the short end of the straw until it fits.

5 Once you have right fit, screw the cap onto the top of the bottle. Place the short end of the bendy straw through the hole.

6 Start blowing into the straw (the end opposite the bottle) and place the ping-pong ball over the stream of air. Observe what happens!

HOW DOES IT WORK?

This is an example of Bernoulli's Principle, the same principle that allows heavier-than-air objects, like airplanes, to fly. Daniel Bernoulli, an 18th century Swiss mathematician, found that the faster air flows over the surface of something, the less the air pushes on that surface. That means that the air pressure on the object is lower than average.

The air from the straw produces the levitating ball phenomenon using Bernoulli's Principle. The fast air that you are blowing around the sides of the ball is at a lower pressure than the surrounding, stationary air. If you look closely, you'll see that the ball wobbles while it is levitating in midair. The ball is attempting to leave the area of low pressure, but the higher air pressure surrounding it forces it back into the low pressure area.

DID YOU KNOW?
Daniel Bernoulli published his "flying" principle in 1738, but the Wright Brothers did not make their first successful plane flights until 1903.

Bubble Snakes

Make your own soapy serpent!

MATERIALS

- Food coloring (optional)
- Bowl of bubble solution - see page 117
- Washcloth(s)
- Empty water bottle
- Adult supervision
- Rubber band
- Utility blade

LET'S EXPERIMENT

DID YOU KNOW?

Bubbles are usually formed when a thin film of liquid surrounds a pocket of air. But there is also such a thing as an "antibubble," which is a thin film of air surrounding liquid. These form when a liquid droplet surrounded by air presses through the surface of more liquid.

1 Following the directions on page 117, use 2–3 tablespoons of dish soap and 9 ounces of water to make a small batch of bubble solution.

2 Find a clean, empty plastic bottle. Ask an adult for help and carefully cut the bottom off of the plastic bottle.

3 Cover the hole with a piece of fabric that is similar to a washcloth or cotton sock. Use a rubber band to keep the fabric in place.

4 If you want colored bubbles, find some liquid food coloring in your favorite color(s). Add a few drops of the food coloring to the fabric on the end of your bottle.

5 Dip the fabric-covered end of the bottle into the bowl of bubble solution.

6 Blow into the mouth of the plastic bottle to make your own Bubble Snakes! Use a fresh washcloth to make more colors.

HOW DOES IT WORK?

Bubbles form because of the surface tension of water. Hydrogen atoms in one water molecule are attracted to oxygen atoms in other water molecules. They like each other so much, they cling together.

When you blow air through your Bubble Snake-maker, you are creating hundreds of tiny bubbles. As the air wiggles through the fabric, bubbles are continuously being made. The bubbles attach to each other when they come out of the fabric. It's all thanks to the same hydrogen bonds that make bubbles possible!

Disappearing Color Wheel

Spin the wheel to see the light!

MATERIALS

- Styrofoam® or paper plate
- Markers (red, orange, yellow, green, blue, purple)
- Glue
- Ruler
- Pencil
- Scissors
- String
- Cardboard
- Plastic cup

LET'S EXPERIMENT

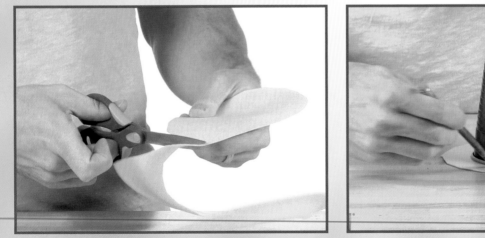

1 Use the scissors to cut the edge off of the disposable plate.

2 On the flat piece of plate, trace the mouth of the cup with a pencil.

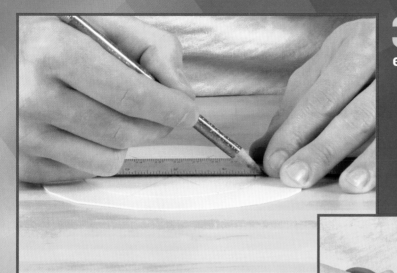

3 Use a ruler and pencil to divide the circle into six even sections.

4 Color each of the six sections a different color using your markers, then cut out the circle.

5 Use the cup to trace a circle on cardboard and cut it out with the scissors, gluing the colored circle and cardboard together. Make sure the colored side faces out!

Disappearing Color Wheel

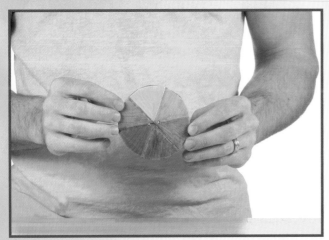

6 Poke two small holes through the wheel near the center of the circle.

7 Cut a 36-inch piece of string. Feed the string through both holes and tie the ends together. (Tip: Use a needle or paperclip if it's difficult to feed the string through the hole.)

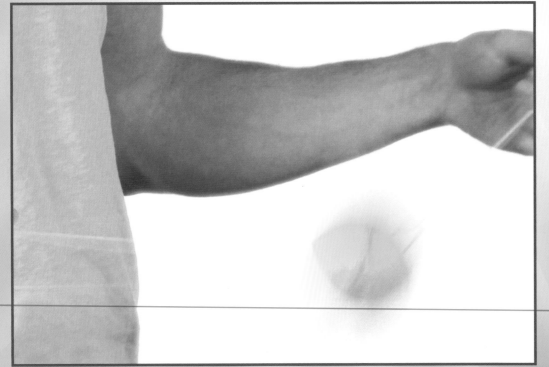

8 Wind the string by moving the wheel in a motion similar to a jump rope.

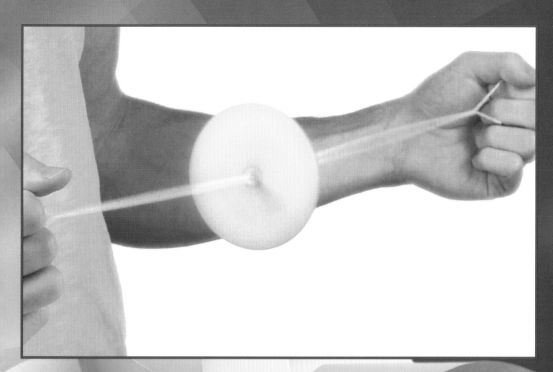

9 Pull the string tight to get the wheel spinning. As the wheel spins, what do you notice about the colors?

TAKE IT FURTHER
Test this experiment with more colors. Will it work if you use black, gray or brown?

HOW DOES IT WORK?

The colors are all still there—they've just mixed together. The rapid spinning of the Disappearing Color Wheel causes the colors to "blend" into each other. This blending creates the illusion that they're actually white! This happens because light is all of the colors in one: white. When the wheel spins up to the right speed, the colors blend into a near-recreation of white light. You see a "white" wheel because your eyes cannot keep up with the rapid rate at which the individual colors are spinning!

DID YOU KNOW?
Humans can't see ultraviolet light, but many kinds of insects can.

127

Magic Tube

We bet you won't be able to tear these tissues!

MATERIALS

- Tissue
- Toilet paper roll
- Wooden dowel
- Rubber band
- Salt

LET'S EXPERIMENT

1 Place one tissue over one end of the toilet paper roll. Secure the tissue in place with a rubber band.

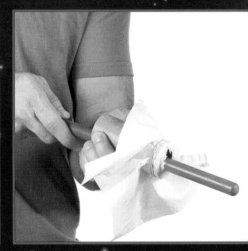

2 Try puncturing the tissue using a wooden dowel or the handle of a wooden spoon. As you probably would have guessed, it tears very easily.

3 Place a new piece of tissue over the end of the toilet paper roll. Once again, secure it with a rubber band. Stand the roll up on a flat surface with the tissue on the bottom.

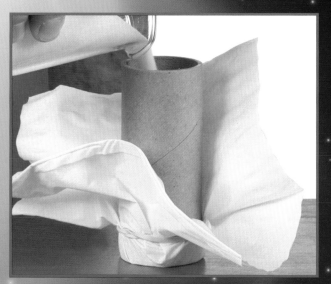

4 Pour salt into the toilet paper roll until the roll is 3/4 full with salt.

5 Lightly tap the toilet paper roll on a hard surface to help pack the salt.

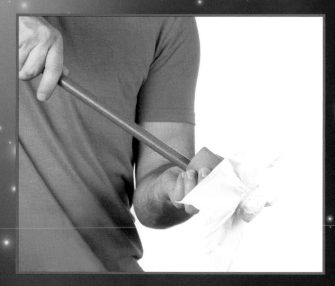

6 Again, try to push the dowel through the tissue on the end. It's practically impossible!

HOW DOES IT WORK?

The key to the tissue's newfound strength is the addition of salt. The hundreds of thousands of salt grains offer much more surface area to dissipate the force you thrust into the tube. As the force spreads from grain to grain of salt (and against the outside of the tube), the force is also spread across the entire area of the tissue. The increased surface area makes the tissue appear much stronger than before!

TAKE IT FURTHER
Fill the toilet paper roll with different materials, like gravel, beads or beans. Which works best?

DID YOU KNOW?
The adult human body contains about 250 grams of salt–that's nearly half a pound.

Balancing Nails

MATERIALS

• Adult supervision

• Hammer

• 12 identical nails

• Wood block

LET'S EXPERIMENT

With an adult's help, carefully hammer one of the nails into the center of the block of wood. It's a good idea to measure and pre-drill the hole to avoid splitting the wooden block. It's important that this nail be standing as straight as possible.

130

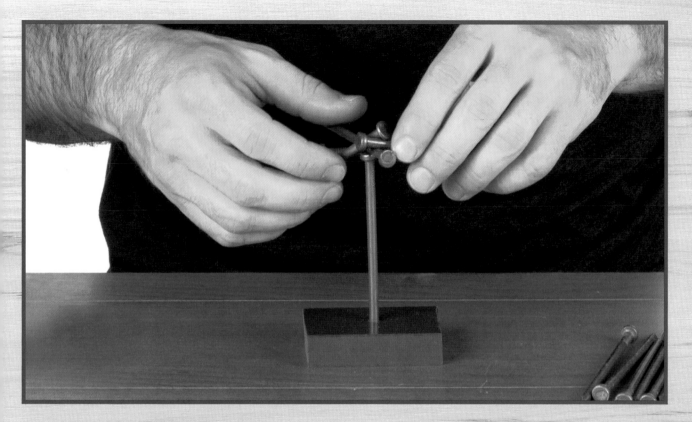

2 Place the wood block flat on a desk or table. The challenge is to balance all of the nails on the standing nail in the wooden block. To win the challenge, none of the 11 nails may touch the wood block, the desk or table, or anything else that might help hold them up. No additional equipment other than the wood block and the nails may be used. See if you can think of some ways to do this and test them out before reading the next step.

DID YOU KNOW?
Humans began attaching rocks to sticks and using them as hammers around 30,000 B.C.

DON'T LOOK YET!
The solution is on the next page, so give yourself a chance to solve the challenge first. Hint: Try to make the nails as symmetrical as possible.

Balancing Nails

3 Lay one nail on a flat surface and place the other nails across this nail, head to head as shown in the photograph above. Finally, place another nail on top of this assembly, head to tail with the second nail.

HOW DOES IT WORK?

Gravity pulls any object toward the center of the Earth as if all of its weight were concentrated at one point. That point is called the center of gravity. Objects fall over when their center of gravity is not supported. For symmetrical objects like a ball or a meter stick, the center of gravity is exactly in the middle of the object. For objects that are not symmetrical, like a baseball bat, the center of gravity is closer to the heavier end. The stability of the nails depends on their center of gravity being right at or directly below the point where they rest on the bottom nail. Add too many nails to the left or right and they become unstable and fall off.

4 Carefully, pick up the assembly and balance it on the upright nail.

TAKE IT FURTHER
Remove one nail at a time. How many can you take away before it falls apart?

Huff and Puff Challenge

Blowing something into a bottle should be easy, right?

MATERIALS

- Small paper ball
- 1-liter bottle
- Straw
- Assorted small objects (paper ball, popcorn, foil ball, etc.)

DID YOU KNOW?
Popcorn kernels can jump up to 3 feet when they're popping.

LET'S EXPERIMENT

1 Create a small ball by crumpling up a piece of paper. The ball needs to be able to loosely sit inside the mouth of the bottle. Place the paper ball in the mouth of a 1-liter bottle that has been placed on its side.

2 Direct a straw toward the mouth of the bottle and attempt to blow the paper ball into the bottle.

3 Watch as the paper ball wiggles and jiggles around before flying out of the bottle!

4 Replace the paper ball with a similar object, like a piece of popcorn, and try again. It won't go in the bottle either. Why not?

HOW DOES IT WORK?

The secret is inside the bottle. Although we refer to the bottle as being "empty," it's actually full to the brim with air. Trying to blow more air into the bottle is impossible.

While you can't blow air into the bottle, you are moving quite a bit of air along the sides of the bottle. When the air blows past the mouth of the bottle, it creates an area of low pressure behind it. This is called Bernoulli's principle. This area of low pressure is exactly what the paper ball needs to hop out of the bottle's mouth!

Disappearing Money

Can you explain where the coin "disappears" to?

MATERIALS

- Clear drinking glass
- Saucer or plate
- Penny
- Water

LET'S EXPERIMENT

1 Set a coin on a flat surface like a table or counter. Place the base of a clear drinking glass over the coin.

2 Cover the mouth of the glass with a small plate. Notice how looking in through the side of the glass you can still see the coin.

3 Now, tilt the plate back and fill the glass with water.

4 Once you've filled the glass, replace the saucer. Can you still see the coin through the side of the glass?

5 Take the plate off the glass. Peer straight to the bottom of the glass through the water. Can you see the coin now?

TAKE IT FURTHER

Experiment with different-sized objects and different amounts of water. Do you think you'd be able to see the penny if the glass was only 1/2 full?

DID YOU KNOW?

Rainbows are made when light refracts in a prism! This happens because each color of light has a different wavelength, making them bend at different angles.

HOW DOES IT WORK?

The trick behind the Disappearing Money experiment is the refraction of light. Images that we see are all light rays that reach our eyes. When these light rays travel through air, they experience little or no refraction. That's why you can still see the penny through the side of the empty glass.

When you poured water into the glass and looked from the side, it was as though the penny had disappeared. But really, it was just some bending light rays. After traveling through the water and the side of the glass, none of the rays were able to reach your eyes.

A Bubble Inside a Bubble

...and inside another one!

MATERIALS

- Granulated sugar

- Dish soap

- Tablespoon

- Water

- Scissors

- Cup

- Pipette or straw

LET'S EXPERIMENT

Pour about 8 ounces of warm water into a cup.

2 Add a tablespoon of granulated sugar. In our tests, Dixie Crystals® and Imperial® brand sugars worked best.

3 Add 2 tablespoons of dish soap to the water. Gently stir until the sugar dissolves. Note: If you can, cover the bubble solution with plastic wrap and let it sit for 24 hours to strengthen. You can still do this activity right away, though!

4 Use the scissors to cut off about 1/2 inch (1 cm) from the bulb end of the pipette. This is now your bubble wand. Alternatively, you can use a straw.

A Bubble Inside a Bubble

5 Choose a flat work surface with no pits or bumps. Smoothness makes better bubbles! That's why it's also important all of the sugar be dissolved in the soap solution. Use your fingers to spread some of the bubble solution in an 8–10-inch (20–25-cm) circle on the work surface of your lab.

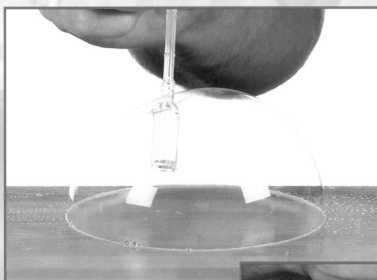

6 Dip the cut end of the bubble wand (the pipette) into the soap solution so it's coated completely. Blow slowly and watch a bubble hemisphere grow onto the moistened surface. Make it a fairly large bubble. The sugar you added gives the bubble wall a lot more strength, flexibility and stability.

7 Dip and coat the bubble wand completely again and gently push it inside the first bubble. Blow a second bubble on the surface inside the first bubble.

8 Take your time and keep blowing bubbles. Always blow a new bubble inside the smallest bubble. As you blow, watch how the outer bubbles change. Think about how each bubble has to accommodate the air trapped inside it with each new bubble you blow.

HOW DOES IT WORK?

Regular bubbles burst when they come in contact with just about anything. Why? A bubble's worst enemies are oil, dirt and gravity. A "sugar" bubble will last a long time on a surface if the surface is free of oil or dirt particles that would normally break through or dissolve the soap film. It's also easier to slip a bubble solution-covered bubble wand or straw through a bubble-try it with a dry one and the bubble will pop.

When you blow a bubble inside a bubble, you probably noticed the outer bubble expanding a little. The additional air not only causes the creation of the inner bubble, it forces the outer bubble to expand to accommodate the inner bubble's volume as well. Thanks to the soapy and sugary solution, the hydrogen bonds in the water are elastic enough to allow for the increase in volume and compression.

DID YOU KNOW?

A 2012 study by the U.S. Agriculture Department found Americans eat an average of 76.7 pounds of sugar per year!

Weekend Wonders

HOMEMADE ROCK CANDY

MAGIC CRYSTAL TREE

These experiments take more than 10 minutes, but they're worth the wait!

MOSS GRAFFITI

IRON FOR BREAKFAST

ICE CREAM!
See page 148 to learn how you can make this sweet treat without any special equipment!

Homemade Rock Candy

It's edible and educational!

MATERIALS

- Cane sugar

- Large glass jar

- Adult supervision

- Medium glass jar

- Water

- Pencil

- Food coloring

- New, clean string

LET'S EXPERIMENT

1 Pour about 3 cups of granulated cane sugar into the large glass container.

2 Add 1 cup (237 mL) of water to the sugar. Watch what happens as the water bubbles through all that sugar. There's a lot going on in the container already. Use a heavy spoon to thoroughly stir the water (a solvent) and the sugar (a solute) together to make a solution. It will be very viscous (thick) and heavy because there's a lot more sugar than water in there. Stir it well!

3 With an adult's help, microwave the solution for 2 minutes on high. (You can use a stove to heat the solution if you prefer.) Heat the solution to the boiling point. Have an adult handle the hot solution and move it to a stable,

heat-safe location. Use a heavy spoon to thoroughly stir the solution again. Make sure all the sugar is stirred, but watch out for splatters of hot liquid. Notice how the solution is changing by just using heat.

4 Move the stirred solution to the microwave (or stove) again and heat it on high for another 2 minutes. Don't let the solution boil over. Again, have an adult move it to a stable, heat-safe location and carefully stir the solution again. It will be more runny than before because of how warm it is.

5 Add three to seven drops of any food coloring to the mixture and stir it in thoroughly.

6 Pour the colored solution into the smaller glass container.

DID YOU KNOW?
Cane sugar has been crystallized by people in India for at least 2,000 years.

Homemade Rock Candy

7 Tie the string to the middle of the pencil. Use the scissors to cut off a length longer than the small container is tall. Lay the pencil on top of the small container and trim the string so it's about 2/3 the height of the container. You want it shorter than the container.

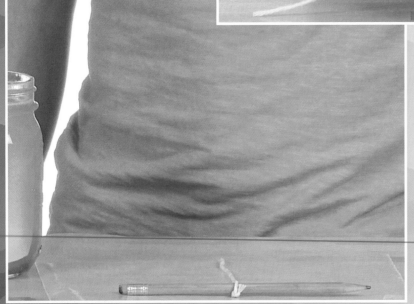

8 Holding the pencil, lower the string into the solution and let it soak for a short time. You want the solution to soak through the string. Lay the pencil and soaked string on a piece of wax paper so the string is perpendicular to the pencil. Allow the solution to cool to room temperature and the straight string to dry completely.

9 Push the dried string into the sugar solution again. You may have to use a slow steady pressure to get it to sink deeply into the solution. You'll need to allow the string to soak in the solution for a week. A paper towel over the container will keep dust out of your experiment. Keep track of changes in the solution and the growing crystals in the solution, but don't disturb them by moving them. Pictures are a good idea!

10 When you're ready for the big reveal, lift the pencil and pull the string loaded with crystals out of the jar. Lay them on some wax paper and look closely at what grew on the string before tasting it!

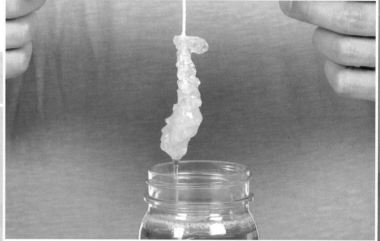

HOW DOES IT WORK?

When you mixed the sugar with the water and then heated and stirred the solution repeatedly, you created a supersaturated solution. This means there are far more dissolved particles of solute (the sugar) than the solvent (the water) can normally dissolve and hold at a given temperature. As the water cools, the sugar falls out of the solution as a precipitate (particles). These connect with other sugar particles and a crystal begins to grow.

You gave the suspended sugar particles a great place to begin crystallizing when you dried some crystals onto the string ahead of time. These are "seed" crystals. As sugar particles begin to settle (the precipitate), they join and form crystals quickly with other sugar molecules.

Homemade Ice Cream

This sweet treat is worth the wait!

MATERIALS

- Gloves
- 1-gallon plastic jar
- Crushed ice
- Rock salt
- 2 food storage bags
- Half-and-half
- Sugar
- Vanilla extract

LET'S EXPERIMENT

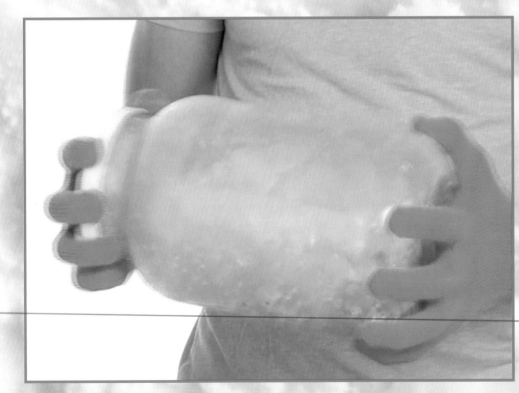

Fill the container about half-full with crushed ice. Add about 6 tablespoons of rock salt to the ice. Seal it and shake the ice and salt combo for about 5 minutes. You'll need to wear your gloves when you're handling the jar—the salt and ice mixture gets down to about 14 degrees F (-10 degrees C)!

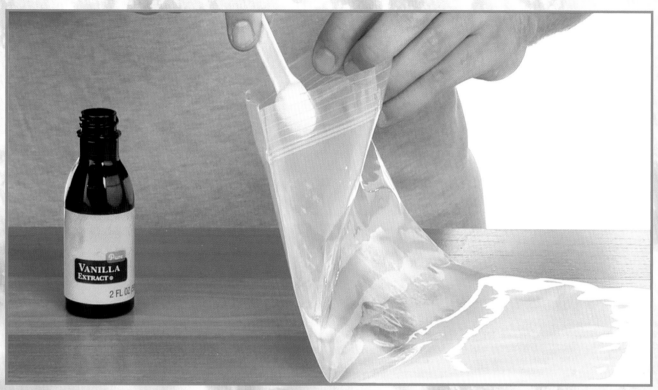

2 Mix the following ingredients in one of the food storage bags:
1/2 cup half-and-half
I tablespoon granulated sugar
1/2 teaspoon vanilla extract

3 Push as much air out of the bag as you can before sealing it tightly. Too much air left inside may pop the bag open during the shaking. Seal the first bag into the second bag by pushing out the air as well. By double-bagging, the risk of salt water and ice leaking into the ice-cream mix is minimized. Place the two sealed bags into the ice and salt mixture. Close the container tightly.

Homemade Ice Cream

4 Wrap the container in the towel or put on your gloves. Shake, rock 'n' roll and mix that container! Your ice cream should be ready after about 15–20 minutes so pace your shaking energy and ask a friend to take a turn shaking.

TAKE IT FURTHER

The more salt you add, the lower the freezing point becomes. How quickly can you make ice cream?

HOW DOES IT WORK?

When salt and ice mix, the freezing point of the ice is lowered. By lowering the temperature at which ice freezes, you were able to create an environment in which the cream mixture could freeze at a temperature below 32 degrees F (0 degrees C) and become ice cream. The shaking (or stirring in an ice-cream maker) moves the warmer cream mixture from the inside to the outside of the bag so it can freeze evenly, making a soft and airy ice cream instead of a hard block.

DID YOU KNOW?

Waffle cones were invented when an ice cream vendor at the 1904 St. Louis World's Fair ran out of dishes and rolled up some waffles to serve it in instead.

32 USA

1904 St. Louis World's Fair

1998

Instant-Freeze Water

This experiment is super cool (and cold).

MATERIALS

- 2 bottles of water

- Rock salt

- Big bowl of ice

- Thermometer

DID YOU KNOW?
Water is the only substance on Earth that is naturally found in three states: solid, liquid and gas.

LET'S EXPERIMENT

1 Shove the water bottles in the big bowl of ice, keeping them close to the center of the bowl and surrounded by and buried in ice as much as possible.

2 Scatter a generous amount of rock salt all over the surface of the ice.

3 Insert the thermometer into the ice between the bottles. Monitor the temperature. Over the next half hour, the temperature will fall slowly. Add ice and salt to the container as needed to keep the bottles buried. Watch that thermometer! The temperature in the bowl needs to drop to 17 degrees F. If the water gets too cold, it may freeze prematurely.

4 After the water has been this cold for 10 minutes (and is still a liquid), gently remove a bottle from the ice/salt mixture. Strike the bottom edge of the bottle sharply against the table. Ice crystals may immediately form near the top of the bottle and quickly move down through the liquid. Carefully remove the second bottle and twist open the cap. The same instant freezing will likely occur from the top down.

HOW DOES IT WORK?

You created "supercooled" water by using salt and ice to drop the temperature in the chill mixture below the normal freezing point of water (32 degrees F or 0 degrees C). This is called "freezing point depression."

When water freezes, the molecules come together in a very orderly way and form a crystalline structure. But supercooled liquids need something to kick-start this process and encourage the molecules to organize themselves this way. The shock wave made when you hit the bottle is a good way to get those molecules moving.

Iron for Breakfast

How much metal do you eat?

MATERIALS

- Total® cereal
- Strong magnet
- Plastic bag
- Water

LET'S EXPERIMENT

1 Open the box and pour 1/2 cup cereal into the bag

2 Fill the bag 1/2 of the way with water.

3 Let the water and cereal mixture sit for at least 1 hour.

155

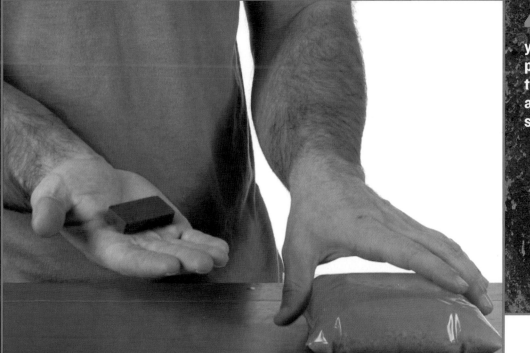

4 Place the magnet in your hand, then place the bag on top. Swish the bag around for 15–20 seconds.

5 Flip the bag over so the magnet is now on top.

6 Examine what has collected beneath the magnet and see if you can move it around.

TAKE IT FURTHER

Test this out with different cereals or other "fortified" foods.

DID YOU KNOW?

Iron is an essential mineral that helps transport oxygen throughout your body. It's also important for keeping your cells, skin, hair and nails healthy.

HOW DOES IT WORK?

Iron is naturally present in many kinds of produce, nuts and meat, and some food manufacturers also add it to cereal because it's a very important part of the human diet. But if you tried to pick up a piece of cereal (or some spinach, another great source of iron) with a magnet, it wouldn't work–there isn't enough iron for the magnetic force to be stronger than the gravity pulling on the cereal. However, cereal and iron do not have the same reaction to water. While the cereal dissolves, the iron does not, making this a good way to separate the bits of iron that are attracted to the magnet.

Magic Crystal Tree

Make a colorful, snow-covered tree.

MATERIALS

- Bowl
- Non-corrugated cardboard
- Mrs. Stewart's® Bluing
- Scissors
- Table salt

- Food coloring

- Water

- Ammonia
- Measuring spoons

LET'S EXPERIMENT

Draw two pine tree shapes onto the cardboard and cut them out.

2 Cut a slot down the middle of one tree shape. Start at the top and stop in the middle of the shape.

3 In the other tree shape, cut a slot up the middle. Start at the bottom and cut to the middle.

4 Slide the two slots together, creating a three-dimensional tree shape that can stand by itself.

Magic Crystal Tree

5 Add drops of food coloring to the edges of the cardboard and let the food coloring soak into the cardboard.

6 Using the bowl, mix these ingredients together:
  1 tablespoon water
  1 tablespoon salt
  1 tablespoon bluing
  1/2 tablespoon household ammonia

7 Stand your tree in the middle of the bowl containing your magic solution. Over the next 10–12 hours, your Magic Crystal Tree will grow and grow and grow! Pretty soon, you'll have a colorful snow-covered tree!

TAKE IT FURTHER

Switch up the amount of salt or change the size or shape of the tree to see how it affects the growth of the crystals. Record what happens each time you change the experiment.

HOW DOES IT WORK?

After the solution has been drawn throughout the tree, it begins to evaporate. The evaporation process is accelerated by the ammonia, which evaporates more quickly than water and leaves behind CRYSTALS.

The crystals are a combination of the Mrs. Stewart's® Bluing (a product that whitens yellowed fabrics by adding blue coloring) and the table salt. The solution you created is supersaturated by the bluing and salt you added to the water. As the bluing and salt water make their way up the tree, the water begins to evaporate, leaving behind the salt and bluing particles to crystallize.

A CRYSTAL is a solid material that forms when molecules fit together in a repeating pattern.

DID YOU KNOW?

Snowflakes are a type of crystal made from ice! They always have six sides, but every snowflake shape is unique.

161

Moss Graffiti

Learn how to grow your own art!

MATERIALS

Adult supervision

Water

Paint brushes

Spray bottle

Moss

Buttermilk

Disposable baby diaper

Blender

Measuring cups

Measuring spoons

Bucket

LET'S EXPERIMENT

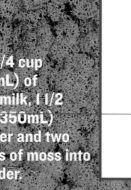

Put 1/4 cup (60mL) of buttermilk, 1 1/2 cups (350mL) of water and two clumps of moss into a blender.

2 Extract the water gel from a baby diaper. You can do this by opening up a new diaper and cutting through the top layer of cotton with scissors. Then shake out the power/gel substance from the inside onto a piece of paper so you can easily collect it.

3 Add 2 teaspoons of the water gel to the blender.

Moss Graffiti

4 Place the lid on the blender and blend until smooth.

5 Pour the moss substance into a bucket that you can use for painting.

DID YOU KNOW?

In World War I, soldiers' wounds were packed with sphagnum moss when bandages became scarce. It worked very well—moss is more absorbent than cotton and has natural antiseptic properties.

6 Ask an adult's permission to paint with the moss substance onto a textured surface, like particle board. Beware of painting on walls, as the moss will remove existing paint. Keep your moss painting in a shady place—moss doesn't like too much sunlight.

7 Keep the moss moist by misting it each day with a spray bottle for several weeks. You may need to mist more often in dry climates. Watch over several weeks as the moss begins to grow!

HOW DOES IT WORK?

Moss is a tiny plant that grows in clumps. Most mosses are made of tiny stems which contain one leaf that is often only one cell thick. Moss also naturally grows in moist, shady spots. Because of this natural preference, keeping the moss moist with a spray bottle is especially important in this activity. The acidity of the buttermilk also helps the moss to grow.

Glossary

ACID A liquid with a lot of hydrogen ions. Acids have a pH between I and 7 and react when mixed with bases.

ADHESION The force that causes two different substances to stick together.

AMPLITUDE A way to measure a sound or light wave. Amplitude describes the height of a wave on a graph.

ATMOSPHERIC PRESSURE The force exerted by air.

BASE A liquid with a lot of hydroxide ions. Bases have a pH between 7 and 14 and react when mixed with acids.

BOILING POINT The temperature at which a liquid boils. Water's boiling point is 212 degrees F (100 degrees C).

BUOYANCY The upward force on an object created by a surrounding gas or liquid.

CARBON DIOXIDE A colorless, odorless gas composed of carbon and oxygen.

CELL The smallest functional unit of an organism.

CENTRIPETAL FORCE A force that pushes an object along a circular path.

CHROMATOGRAPHY Using a solid support (like paper) to separate different kinds of molecules.

COHESION The attraction of like molecules to one another.

CONCAVE Having a surface that curves inward.

CONVEX Having a surface that curves outward.

DECIBEL A unit used to measure the intensity of sound.

DENSITY A measure of how compact a substance is. Density equals mass divided by volume.

DISSOLVE To become incorporated in liquid, forming a solution.

DNA Deoxyribonucleic acid, a material in nearly all living organisms that carries genetic information.

ELECTRON A negatively charged subatomic particle. Electrons carry electricity.

EXPERIMENT A scientific procedure done to test a hypothesis or demonstrate a known fact.

FORCE An influence that changes the motion of a body.

FREEZING POINT The temperature at which a liquid becomes a solid. Water freezes at 32 degrees F (0 degrees C).

FRICTION The resistance that occurs when one object moves over another.

GAS A substance in a state that has no fixed shape or volume and will expand to fill whatever container it is in.

GENE Chromosomal information passed from a parent to their offspring.

GRAVITY The force that attracts everything to the center of the Earth, or any other body with mass.

HEX NUT A nut with a hexagonal (six-sided) shape, meant to be fitted onto a bolt.

HYDROPHILIC Tending to mix with or dissolve in water.

HYDROPHOBIC Tending to repel water.

INDICATOR A chemical that changes color if it comes in contact with an acid or a base.

ION An atom with a positive or negative charge.

Glossary

KINETIC ENERGY The energy of motion; potential energy is converted into kinetic energy as it is used.

LENS A piece of glass with curved sides used to focus or disperse light rays.

LIQUID A substance that flows freely but has constant volume.

MAGNETIC FIELD The area around a magnet which carries the force of magnetism.

MASS A measure of the amount of matter in an object.

MEMBRANE A thin layer of cells or tissue that acts as a boundary within an organism.

MICELLE An electrically charged particle found in solutions such as soaps and detergents.

MOLECULE The smallest unit of a chemical compound that can be part of a chemical reaction.

NEUTRAL A liquid with a pH of 7, like distilled water, is neutral.

NEUTRON A subatomic particle that does not carry an electric charge.

NEWTON'S FIRST LAW OF MOTION Objects at rest tend to stay at rest and objects in motion tend to stay in motion, unless an outside force acts upon them.

NUCLEIC ACID An organic substance commonly found in DNA that is made up of many nucleotides in a long chain.

NUCLEOTIDE A compound that forms the basic structural unit of nucleic acids, like DNA.

OBSERVE To carefully watch the way something is happening.

ORGANISM A living being,

like an animal, plant or single-celled life-form.

PH A measure of hydrogen ion concentration.

PIPETTE A thin tube used for transferring or measuring small amounts of liquid.

POTENTIAL ENERGY The stored energy an object has because of its position or state.

PRESSURE A continuous force exerted on an object.

PROTON A subatomic particle with a positive electric charge.

REACTION A chemical process where two or more substances change one another into different substances.

SOLID A substance with a constant shape and volume.

SOLUBLE Able to be dissolved in water. Something dissolved in water is called a solute.

SOLUTION A liquid mixture where the solute is equally distributed throughout the solvent.

SOLVENT The liquid in which a solute is being dissolved.

SUPERCOOL To cool a liquid below its freezing point without solidification or crystallization.

SURFACE AREA The total area of a surface.

SURFACE TENSION A force in the surface layer of a liquid that causes it to act like an elastic sheet. This is caused by cohesion.

TEMPERATURE A degree of hotness or coldness that can be measured with a thermometer.

THERMOMETER A tool used for measuring temperature.

VOLUME The amount of space taken up by an object.

STEVE SPANGLER—known by fans worldwide for his wildly funny, unconventional and engaging science demonstrations on stage, television and other venues—first came to fame in 2005 with his Mentos Diet Coke Experiment in which he taught millions via YouTube how to turn an ordinary bottle of soda into an erupting geyser of fun. Today, Steve's catalog of videos featured on YouTube have more than 350 million views, and his books and online experiments are widely used by parents and educators to increase student engagement and inspire young scientists to learn more about STEM-based careers.

Spangler is a bestselling author, educator and Emmy award-winning television host who finds the most creative ways to make science fun. With more than 1,300 television appearances and multiple Emmy awards to his credit, Steve is also a regular guest on *The Ellen DeGeneres Show,* where she dubbed him "America's Science Teacher." He hosts his own nationally syndicated television series called *DIY Sci,* where viewers learn how to use do-it-yourself experiments to amaze friends. Spangler was inducted into the National Speaker Hall of Fame in 2010 and he holds a Guinness World Record for conducting the world's largest science experiment in 2009.

To learn more, visit *SteveSpangler.com.*

Media Lab Books
For inquiries, call 646-838-6637

Copyright 2019 Topix Media Lab

Published by Topix Media Lab
14 Wall Street, Suite 4B
New York, NY 10005

Printed in Canada

The information in this book has been carefully researched, and every reasonable effort has been made to ensure its accuracy. Neither the book's publisher nor its creators assume any responsibility for any accidents, injuries, losses or other damages that might come from its use. You are solely responsible for taking any and all reasonable and necessary precautions when performing the activities detailed in its pages.

All rights reserved. No part of this book may be reproduced in any form or by any electronic or mechanical means, including information storage and retrieval systems, without permission in writing from the publisher, except by a reviewer, who may quote brief passages in a review.

Certain photographs used in this publication are used by license or permission from the owner thereof, or are otherwise publicly available. This publication is not endorsed by any person or entity appearing herein. Any product names, logos, brands or trademarks featured or referred to in the publication are the property of their respective trademark owners. Media Lab Books is not affiliated with, nor sponsored or endorsed by, any of the persons, entities, product names, logos, brands or other trademarks featured or referred to in any of its publications.

ISBN-13: 978-1-948174-11-4
ISBN-10: 1-948174-11-1

CEO Tony Romando

Vice President & Publisher Phil Sexton
Senior Vice President of Sales & New Markets Tom Mifsud
Vice President of Retail Sales & Logistics Linda Greenblatt
Director of Finance Vandana Patel
Manufacturing Director Nancy Puskuldjian
Financial Analyst Matthew Quinn
Brand Marketing & Promotions Assistant Emily McBride

Editor-in-Chief Jeff Ashworth
Creative Director Steven Charny
Photo Director Dave Weiss
Managing Editor Courtney Kerrigan
Senior Editor Tim Baker

Content Editor Kaytie Norman
Content Photo Editor Catherine Armanasco
Art Director Susan Dazzo
Assistant Art Director Michelle Lock
Associate Editor Trevor Courneen
Copy Editor & Fact Checker Benjamin VanHoose

Co-Founders Bob Lee, Tony Romando

For Smithsonian Enterprises
President Carol LeBlanc
Vice President Brigid Ferraro
Director of Licensed Publishing Jill Corcoran
Senior Manager Licensed Publishing Ellen Nanny
Product Development Manager Kealy Gordon

Thank you to Smithsonian reviewer:
Tim Pula, Interpretive Exhibits Inventor
Spark!Lab, Smithsonian

All Steve Spangler portraits and step-by-step images Courtesy Steve Spangler Science. All art Shutterstock except; p2 TOLBERT PHOTO/Alamy; p6 heshphoto/Getty Images; p9 Gabriel (Gabi) Bucataru/Stocksy; p13 vernonwiley/iStock; p15 Steve Debenport/iStock; p17 PrairieArtProject/iStock; p25 Diana Walker//Time Life Pictures/Getty Images; p29 Dejan Ristovski/Stocksy; p36 Bulkley Valley Museum (2); p48 lenscap67/iStock; p56 David Kohl/AP Images; p57 Courtesy Library Of Congress; p67 chaimdan/iStock; p71 Pictorial Press Ltd/Alamy; p81 INTERFOTO/Alamy; p87 Courtesy Yann Caradec/Wikimedia Commons, Courtesy Antoine-Francaois Called/Wikimedia Commons; p99 Aleksandr Belgian/Alamy; p121 Courtesy Wellcome Collection; p143 chuckcollier/iStock; p158 Catherine Armanasco/Topix Media Lab

© 2019 Topix Media © 2019 Smithsonian Institution.

©2019 Smithsonian Institution. The name "Smithsonian" and the Smithsonian logo are registered trademarks owned by the Smithsonian Institution.

Smithsonian

The experiments presented herein were originally featured on Steve Spangler's Sick Science YouTube channel.